Katia Ricklin

I live to realize that I realize all there is myself

novum pro

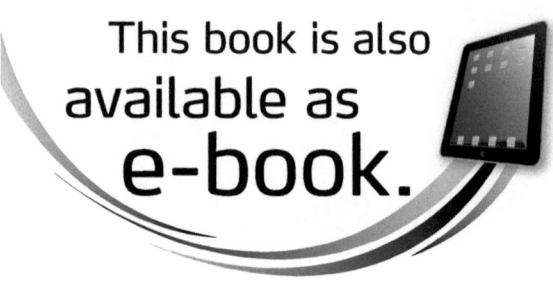

All rights of distribution, including via film, radio, and television, photomechanical reproduction, audio storage media, electronic data storage media, and the reprinting of portions of text, are reserved.

© 2021 novum publishing

ISBN 978-3-99107-337-6
Cover photo: Katia Ricklin
Cover design, layout & typesetting: novum publishing
Internal illustrations: Katia Ricklin

www.novumpublishing.com

Contents

Pre-Word 7

YOU LIVE TO REALIZE THAT YOU REALIZE ALL THERE IS YOURSELF

The big question WHY 17
Splitting / Diversion / Separation 21
Becoming conscious 27
The principle of polarity 30
Reality – the outside 37
Unipolar one-sidedness 41
Mirror of yourself 43
Death 45
Thoughts, beliefs, and behavior patterns 47
The Word 53
Self-recognition aids 57
The Senses 61
Realization through physical and
    psychological problems 71
Bach flowers 84
Crystals, colors, and diseases 86
The connection of planets and colors 96
Tarot 104
The 4 elements 106
Astrological Circle 110
Earth 118
Bach flower texts in connection with the
    western zodiac signs and the Chinese animal signs ... 120
The way of life in the Tarot 127
Numbers and the way of life 135
A = 0 (zero) 140

Pre-Word

I experienced the happiest times of my childhood with my mother's parents in Lucerne. Both were surgeons and lived in a large apartment with an integrated medical practice together with Miss Lendi, the practice assistant, and Nina, who was responsible for the household and also cooked. Whenever my grandparents came to Zurich, I was ready with my little suitcase to go away with them because I felt well and fully taken. I was their sunshine and brightened their busy day. My grandpa was always in the clinic in the morning operating, and my grandma in the doctor's office. I was allowed to help: In a white nurse's apron with a small red cross on it, I opened the door and led the patients into the waiting room. When patients had to have x-rays, I held their arms or legs and helped Miss Lendi hang the pictures on a leash in a darkened bathroom after development to dry. In the afternoon, Omi took me shopping or for a dog walk by the lake. Before dinner, I filled golden or silver tin cans with 'special' ointments and helped roll back washed bandages. After dinner, I went with Miss Lendi to get newspapers and cigarettes for Grandpa.

My Omi told me a lot about her experiences in her youth and her travels in the Orientexpress. She was born in Bulgaria and grew up there. Around 1910, when she was 17, she decided to study medicine in France. Her openness for new people and environments, which she 'mirrored' me, helped me a lot in my further life. But not only her courage and her spirit of adventure fascinated me, but also her sensitive and spiritual nature. She laid cards and knew in advance when my brother or I would get sick. It was an exceptional atmosphere in Lucerne, and I was absolutely happy.

When I was seven years old, this wonderful time ended because I had to go to school. In the first grade, I was almost always ill, had kidney problems. I thought about that a lot later, and it became clear to me that I was no longer in harmony with myself. Every night I woke up because my nose was clogged, and I could no longer breathe. I then sat up and waited until the constipation was released. I remember well that every night I asked myself: *Why am I alive?* This question haunted me for years until I was ready to find the answers when I was over forty.

I can hardly remember my school days. It was a time without great ups and downs. My parents and teachers told me what to do and what not to do, and I obeyed.

I broke a leg in a skiing accident shortly before my A-levels. This fact upset my family's daily life for some time. Suddenly I was the main person who my parents and teachers took care of touchingly and carefully. Even my rather bad grades didn't count anymore, and I passed the final exams without any problems. Today I am convinced that my inner baby, as I always call it, had helped me with the accident to simplify this difficult time.

I was almost 20 years old and had to decide on an education. Actually, like my grandparents and father, I wanted to study medicine. But then, in 1967, there was a general opinion that it was pointless for a girl to start studying because she would soon get married anyway. In Switzerland, there was not even the women's right to vote these times...

After studying history for 2 years, I decided to study English in Cambridge to free myself from my parents and to meet new people, make new experiences. After half a year, I returned to Zurich with a diploma as an English teacher, an education that I complemented with a secretary course, which helped me a lot later. Living with my parents again was even more difficult than before because they still treated like a child again. Since I did not know better, I again played this role, not yet being aware of my inner power.

But then a light came on – a door opened. Friends of my parents had emigrated to the Bahamas and invited us. How beautiful these days were: the turquoise sea, the white beaches, the sun, and the warmth – it flooded my body and soul. It was 'next to paradise', and I was happier than I had been for a long time. I felt at home, and I realized what life could be like. Owanta and Einar were lovable, cheerful, and took me in their arms at the first hello. Although at the age of my parents, they became real friends. Once again, my inner Self assisted me in opening up new sides of me, this time for love and affection. From that moment on, I traveled to see them whenever I could manage to escape from my 'normal' life – it must have been over 70 times until they passed away. They treated me like a part of the family and took me along where ever they would go. I learned to catch fish, to clean them, to drive boats and trucks or to plant palm trees and other beautiful plants. It so much reminded me of my happy days I spent with my grandparents: I felt accepted and valuable.

I still have close contact with the son and the daughter of Owanta and Einar and go to visit them regularly.

One year after my first trip to the Bahamas I married the man whom I had met 2 years before in Zurich. Right at the beginning of our marriage, I already knew that he was not the dream partner for a lifetime, but I had the chance to leave my childhood behind and to become an adult. Through his job, we were able to part and live in Morristown in the States for a year. Since our home only was one hour away from New York, we almost every Sunday drove there mainly to meet an old Swiss friend who was seriously sick lying in a hospital. The relation between him and me became very close, and we both cried when it was time for me to leave the States as we 'knew' that we would never see each other anymore.

Our next domicile was Munich in Germany, where my husband started to work as the chef in his father's company. As in the States, I took care of the household, but I began to feel that I missed the challenges in life. Organizing the home, cooking, washing, and going on long walks with our dog did not fill me up anymore. Again there came a change: Mikki, the daughter of Owanta and Einar, came to stay with us for a year while she was studying in Munich. She enlightened my life! Like her parents, she was a patient listener. By talking about my problems, I became aware of the fact that I did not want to end up in the same situation as my mother being 'just' a housewife and undermining my power and my abilities. With Mikki's help, I dared to follow my inner wishes and got divorced in 1974. This decision was a shock to my family as well as a lot of our friends. For me, it meant to stand on my own feet.

I decided to take a 'lower' job in a family-run business dealing with sports articles. Soon I got more demanding tasks, and after a year, I became co-chef at the side of Robert, who became my partner and friend. I not only worked inside the company anymore but had to go out to the front as a salesgirl for a ski- and tennis wear collection that I had to sell to sports shops in Switzerland. Each spring and autumn, a new collection was presented out of which my clients chose the styles and colors and told me how many pieces in what sizes they wanted to order for delivery half a year later to their shops.

I remember very well how nervous I was in the evening before I had to present the collection the first time on an international fair in Munich the next day. In the afternoon, we had had a meeting where the designer presented the ski pants and ski jackets for this new season. My new colleagues who were selling in other countries transmitted some of their experience to me, and I received 5 sheets of paper with sketches, the names, and the prices of the different styles. Was it hard enough to get started I knew that I had to talk to the clients not only in German but in French and Italian as well.... To be informed the next day, I learned the names and prices by heart, which brought me quite a bit of self-security that the clients appreciated the next day. They loved the collection and were willing to give me appointments to place their orders in Switzerland in the coming weeks.

Already in this first season, I made an increase of 400% more than my predecessor. Right at the beginning, I already knew that the result on the paper only was a part of the success as only the sales figures in the shops counted in the end. And it happened, and the success followed every year again.

I cannot say from where it came, but right at the beginning of my job as a salesgirl, I just 'knew' which styles and colors will sell out well. The same kind of 'feeling', 'knowing' I had for the final consumers in the shops by observing my clients when I saw them for the first time. My clients were open to my sights and ordered according to my suggestions, sold very well, and all we were happy. Whenever I talk about these times, I still feel joy and happiness.

It was a long, intense, and very busy time, but I developed myself from a little mouse to an important person – I was proud and it gave me a lot of pleasure. Being completely involved in the company's tasks there were no free evenings nor weekends to think of something else. My private life was at zero as there was no time for friends. For a long time, I did not miss anything as my paradise-like trips to the Bahamas three times a year filled the gap.

One day my dearest grandmother died. When I got this message, I started to cry and was very sad until an inner voice asked me what I was crying for. She urged me to recognize that all my sentences began with 'I': I cannot see you again. I feel bad that I have not visited you regularly lately. I will not learn more from you, etc. I asked the voice what I should do, and the answer was that I should send positive words to her and imagine how she happily passes into a new dimension. By doing this, the grieve faded, and I, in a way, felt enlighted. Thinking of her, I suddenly was sure that the spirituality she had mirrored to me already was in me, which explained my ability of foresight.

The day after her death, I went to town and found a book for laying and reading the French cards like my Omi used to do… It was incredible!

My intensive work with the cards brought more and more of my and other's unconsciousness into the light. What I realized the most was: there was much more behind reality, and there definitely was a sense of life.

A few years after Omi's death, Gerda came into my life. She was 'special', different then all the other people I knew. She used the pendulum to predict, foresaw things that sometimes materialized, and some other times not – she just was in a way 'lifted' from reality and did not stand on the earth with her 2 feet. Still, her way of thinking interested me, and I searched more to find answers to the supernatural and the mystery behind reality.

1984 was an eventful year. In January, the warehouse burnt down what brought the company in financial straits. In May, my partner Robert who was boat racing, rolled over with his boat at a race on the Seine river in Paris and broke a neck vertebra that made him stay in the hospital for 5 months. This accident made me take over even more responsibility – I was in charge of 30 employees and 17 suppliers I had to visit. New doors opened, and this resulted in exciting trips to not only European countries and the Bahamas but to South Korea and Hong Kong on my own. In this same year, I met an American, a former pilot, while I was on vacation in the Bahamas. Dave mostly lived on his houseboat or in his house on a small island where there only were 5 houses in total. One evening the two of us were invited at his neighbor, Frank. On the entrance hall, there was a hook with the red floppy hat of his already dead predecessor.

Frank brought up the story that he and other men (only men) sometimes were able to see the older man walking on the beach with his dog. Every time they saw this vision, the hat was wet the next morning, leaving a puddle on the floor.

Another story of the same category I heard from Dave: In 1972, an Eastern Air Lines plane crashed in the Everglades in Florida, and most of the passengers died. This technician whose fault it had been suddenly showed up in other Eastern Air Lines flights whenever there was a problem and told the crew that this or that would happen and that the pilots should land at once. He also warned the crews of a Delta airplane. His face and voice popped up out of the oven that formerly had been in the crashed aircraft. He was real, and it all always happened as he had predicted.

Shortly later, I read an incredible story in the newspaper. There were many accidents on a major highway in Switzerland with many dead people. A young girl survived while her parents died and had to stay in the hospital for a while. A reporter heard that she was always talking about a hay wagon and interviewed her. She told him that out of a sudden this hay wagon was in front of her father's car. On it was a man fidgeting with a pitchfork. The accident happened because her father changed into the left-hand lane. The reporter searched for answers. He found out that this dead farmer had been fighting years ago because the landmark on his property had been placed incorrectly. The government took notice and after the correct setting of the landmark, there were no accidents anymore… All these mystical stories made me go more in-debth into wanting to know more regarding what is life and reality about and made me inquisitorial about what else I will find on my way.

Working became much more relaxed the 4 following years, although I made some odd experiences. I got sour that my partner more and more retreated from the company and only criticized the employees and me when he showed up. It was funny, but I developed a craving for lemons at this time. Shortly after, I got a terrible rash on my face. Nobody was able to explain this to me or advise me on what to change. Only 2 years later, I figured that it could be the lemons, I stopped eating them, and the rash was gone. Once again, it was my inner baby who wanted to make me aware that I was inwardly allergic what made me have the allergy on the outside.

This was not the only hint of my inner Self that I should change my life: As in every half year, 1988 came the sport's fair in Munich up again. I did not honestly want to go but did not dare to say so. One week before departure, I 'materialized' severe pneumonia that made me stay at home. In these 2 weeks of resting, it suddenly came to my mind that there was no way to go on in this company as it took my breath away and that I had to resign. After having been rooted in a company for a long time and having given your energy for it, the termination is no walk in the park. But the signs of my body were so violent as well as the external circumstances dealing with the company were so distorted that I didn't want to crawl back. I resigned and opened myself to new unknown experiences.

A new recently divorced man stepped into my life with whom I had an intense short relationship. He had two daughters, with whom we spent quite a lot of time and often discussed over their little problems. The contact with them and the children of my cousin was the beginning of a good relationship with young people. Still, up to now, children and youngsters love to come and talk to me. Their reality is not so strongly focused on the matter; understanding and respect take on a much greater significance. They zap around the television programs without distinguishing whether what they see is 'true' or just a story. Children are still very free, only gradually do they get used to the rules of the material world and adopt them.

At this time, I often helped people of different ages who had problems and used the Bach Flowers and the Tarot Cards as an aid. It was interesting that the 'patients' all changed during the conversation when they recognized their problems by the texts of Dr. Bach and the cards.

At that time, I once sat on the balcony with my friend reading a book concerning problems. It said that the parents were to blame for every issue of a person. The statement made me sensitive – my nose had been stuffy for over 40 years, and I always had a spray with me to get air. I tried to connect my problem with myself and my parents and remembered that in my childhood, I had never dared to speak. My inner voice told me that from now on, I should breathe and express my opinion and wishes aloud. Before falling asleep, I said the words: From tomorrow, my nose will be open. You won't believe it, but my nose was 'open' the next day! As a result, I had to be very careful not to fall into the old habit of silence, but to stand courageously by myself and speak out.

Over the next few years, I became more and more involved with tarot, crystals, Bach flowers – all aids to learning more about the 'behind the scenes'. Returns to past lives also seemed exciting to me – but I quickly realized that they showed me the current state from a different 'point of view' to wake me up, to become aware of what was no longer 'right' in my life so that I could change something.

And then something 'strange' happened again: I attended a meditation course for ten weeks, which took place on Wednesday evening. In between, I traveled to the Bahamas for two weeks. We agreed that the course participants telepathically 'sent' me a message on the first Wednesday. And I should send them something equally on the second Wednesday. My disappointment was quite high when I didn't 'receive' anything. On the return flight, I had an extended stay in Miami, where I spent time in an airport bar. Five minutes before the call that the plane was ready to board, I had the idea to buy something in a souvenir shop. There I saw magnet shells, of which I bought ten without questioning myself. Back home, a friend came to visit me. I wanted to give her two of these shells when a student of the class called and asked me to my astonishment if I had brought something with me. It turned out that the meditation group, which consisted of ten people, had telepathically sent me the message that I should bring a shell to each one … The meditation group had received from me that I was freezing and had to warm myself with a fur coat. That was my inner mood because there was a cold feeling between my friend and me. The separation was the logical consequence.

In 1990 I was asked by the Volkshochschule Stäfa whether I would give a course on Bach flowers. That was too 'narrow' for me. I went to bed with the question of what I wanted to talk about in a course, and the next morning I woke up with the idea of calling the course 'We live to become conscious'. The organizer agreed, and I began to prepare myself intensively. I tried to find a common denominator for the different tools, the Bach flowers, the crystals, the astrology, and the Tarot cards with the theme of my course – unbelievable doors opened for me. It seemed *to me as if my brain was a sieve; I was running out white antennas, which made the connections 'simple'. Everything I wanted to talk about suddenly fitted together; in other words, all the aids brought me to the same realization: that we should become conscious of our spiritually incomprehensible being through our life in the material world. That here on the polar reality, we should learn to grasp that we ourselves create the outside. And that we can change this outside at any time if we become conscious of our unconscious sides, our inner being. Furthermore, it became clear to me that in the end, we will return to our original spiritual state, where the ego will unite with everything like a drop in the sea and become all one.*

I noticed during my preparations, that time could be short. The registration for the course ran out, there were nine, although I had 35 'noses' in my head. It was 'remarkable' that two weeks later there were suddenly 35 interested people and no restaurant could be found for November. The course took place in January 1991 and had 32 participants – together with me and my dogs 35 noses filled the hall ...

After the course, a participant advised me to record these findings in a book, which I did. Now I had to put the different topics I had addressed in the course into context and on paper. A neighbor lent me a computer, a very advanced text machine at the time. I sat in front of it, and my fingers began to write... The texts and with it many other connections bubbled – was that me? – into the computer and materialized through the printer in black and white. I can only describe this experience in such a way that I acted as a medium and that spiritual wisdom, foreign to me at that time, was expressed through my writing fingers. An 'it' made itself feel as an inaudible voice that 'dictated' the texts and drawings to me. I did not ask conscious questions – the answers to my original question: 'Why do I live?' just came. It was incredible.

Since then, such pearls of wisdoms have stepped and still step into my consciousness and my life. First, they have to be 'digested', and then through the experience, the certainty builds up that they are right and that life changes enormously through them. At that time, I had no idea how much this new view was true in my life.

The wisdom written down in 1991 was buried in my closet for years until two years ago, a seeress told me I was a medium ... I mentioned the manuscript, and she encouraged me to revise it and make it public. She stressed: The time has come and many people are open to change.

What you learn and read in this book are the texts that were visible on paper at the time. To make them more pictorial, I have added some experiences and insights. You will certainly, like me, open your eyes and ears, and you will realize that you yourself realize your life, your existence and can change it by uniting the 'I' and your inner Self. You, too, will receive answers to the questions: Why am I? What is the meaning of life?

YOU LIVE TO REALIZE THAT YOU REALIZE ALL THERE IS YOURSELF

The big question WHY

You search the answers for the big question, WHY? – the sense behind life.

The answers essentially are all in yourself and your subjectively perceived reality.

Realize that you are the center of everything and that you realize your reality yourself!
You are responsible for your life and your experiences!

There is nothing in your life that does not make sense. All that is comes from your inside – you materialize it to become conscious of the immense unconscious Self that you are, from where you came and where you will go. The moment you want to change yourself and your life, you have to understand your inner world by focusing on the outside that is full of symbols and mirrors, your original wisdom.

Let you lead in this world now by throwing an eye on the history of creation:

In the bible, you read that God created man in his image. You, therefore, are the image of God and the impersonation of the divine and intangible overall. But you are not conscious of this. Everything is in yourself! There is no God beyond – you yourself are the creator of your reality. And therefore everybody himself is responsible for what is befalling him. It is on you to find back to your origin where all is one by becoming aware of your holistic Self and by understanding your existence in polarity.

In the bible, it also says that you were 'tempted' and thrown out of paradise to become aware. You were inquisitive and started your life searching for the reason of you being alive. From this moment on, you separated the holy 'paradise' from the world, the reality with good and evil, black and white, you and me. In Latin 'par' means equal, equivalent, or parallel – therefore, you will find paradise nowhere else than here and now. Your goal is to merge, to mate the two poles!

With your birth, you stepped out of spirituality, the nescience into another dimension, the polarity. You yourself wanted to become conscious of this immense and wonderful being that you are. You decided to go through a polar system to enlighten your inner spiritual Self and finally become one and holistic again. On this side, there is nothing without the other pole. There is no day without the night, no cold without warm, no in without out. You cannot recognize light if you do not know the dark. You chose this path – now is the time to start realizing that the outside, the matter is reflecting your inside and that everything in your reality is connected with you as you yourself create it to grow and augment your knowledge. You will understand more and more when you change your attitude and will be able to look at yourself and the outside from another perspective – from the other side of the visible.

Matter does not exist without the spirit. In your belief, you put the 'spirit' into the other pole. But remember: It is YOU who make the outside out of your beliefs, thought- and behavior patterns that lie hidden inside yourself. Consequently, your subjective reality is the mirror of your inner world!

You are the creator!

To become aware of this immense multidimensional 'I' that you are, you have to start to conceive what the outside is reflecting you – echoing you. Through concentrating on the material side, you will be able to explore your inner mental side. All that is inside reflects on the outside and vice versa, the whole truth, and wisdom. You concentrate only on fragments of the whole and therefore do not see the multidimensional connections. This narrow-minded view makes your daily reality to an illusion. The moment though your inner urge is set free to discover your magnificent and immense Self, you will be open for signs, tools, and people who will help you on your new path of discovery. Your inner fire will encourage you to grow and expand your horizons mentally.

Expansion, however, only can happen through the concentration – the explosion only through implosion. To become aware of this imperceptible mental 'I', you must start to concentrate on yourself and to learn to translate your creations that reflect through your reality. The only way is by asking you: **WHY** do I experience this or that you will get to know yourself. You will realize what you mentally realized, materialized. If you step out into nature, you will see the beauty and the richness inside you. But you will also get the feedback of your beliefs, your thoughts, and your behavior patterns that mirror in the situations you live through. You will be capable of perceiving the self-imposed patterns that are constraining and limiting you and leave them behind. You will then be open for real liberty and happiness – you will create situations filled with pleasure and joy, the explanation of having heaven on earth. On your further path, you will dissolve the densification of matter. You will free yourself of all duration limits and arise in the spiritual sphere from where you originally came. There you will be unconditionally free again with no limits, no time, no space – all is one, all is now, and all is possible!

Your original Self has everything in itself. But you were not conscious of your wholeness because you did not have the other pole.

You, therefore, decided yourself to step out of the chaotic spiritual sphere and to live through the other logical pole of matter to become conscious – conscious of your immortal and multidimensional 'I' and aware that every little thought changes all.

Therefore you created this other pole – to step out of the fog and enlighten the wonders that lie in yourself. You wanted to go through a process of learning through experiences and interchange of thoughts to finally realize that matter is the mirror of spirit – the all-embracing consciousness.

Splitting / Diversion / Separation

By the jump into this-worldliness, the moment of your birth, you wandered step by step, year by year into the pole of matter, and split your multidimensional being and knowing into all manifestation. You were not aware of the fact that all that you see and hear from day one of your life is part of your true Self and that you consequently separated yourself as 'I' from your wholly Self. On this path, pictures and voices on the outside fascinated you, and you started to believe that these projections of yourself are real. When you began to give the outside more importance than to yourself, the division between your inside and the outside happened – this new consciousness separated from the great unconscious. Subsequently, you as an 'I' then lost your entity and fell out of the 'androgyne' status that combines the male and the female sides. Adam symbolizes your real being in whom both poles were one at the beginning.

<u>You all were born alone. And it was your will to pass through this world to become conscious of your entity and become 'all-one' again! Life will bring you back to your true Self – to the center that you are!</u>

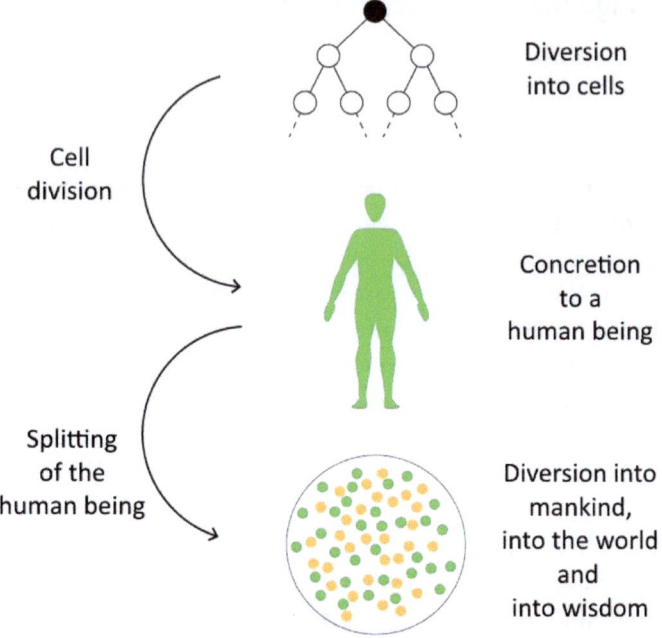

This image of the diversion of the cells will help you understand the splitting of yourself. One original cell divides itself, first in 2, then in 4, in 8, and so forth until this basic unit has divided itself into millions of cells that all carry the same consciousness. However, each of these cells has its own function in the system. The baby comes out of this immense diversity as a human being.

Every single person is a conglomeration of an intangible diversity. Two poles (egg and semen) make the conception: the negative female and receptive pole plus the positive male and urging forward pole. After birth, the same splitting takes place. The baby divides itself into 2 projections – into the female mother and the male father. And then into the 4 grandparents, again female and male parts. Subsequently, there are more and more projections of the baby unit until the outer world reflects all the inner diversity and wisdom.

What you perceive as reality is, in fact, the diversion of your wholly Self – the one and all!

By parting yourself in millions of aspects of yourself and not being aware of this fact, you start to believe that the projections are outside. And by giving them the power, you make yourself little. You listen to the YOU's, become submissive, and lose the belief into yourself. You accept what the parents, teachers, and other people tell you and start subsequently to build up thought- and faith-patterns.

You undermine your own needs as you start:
— To believe that you are only loved and accepted when you do something good
— To give away love obsequiously
— To pass on your energy to others
— To stand up to others
— To show understanding for others
— To listen to others
— To want to be loyal
— To help
— To take over initiatives and responsibility for others
— To pity others
— To take over tasks for others and hence give up yourself.

But also:
— Criticize others
— Get angry at others
— Blame others
— Believe that you are as you are and therefore think that you cannot change your situation.

The threats coming from the outside make you insecure and lets you protect all around you. As you have lost your inner security, you are afraid that the 'outside' could take away precious things like money, healthiness, a beloved person, and finally, your own life. You hold fast onto that what you believe in having in the shine of reality and fight for it because you have lost faith in yourself. You do not dare to let go – you are afraid of death as you do not understand that death is the other pole of life. The old has to dissolve to make room for the new – this happens from one moment to the next!

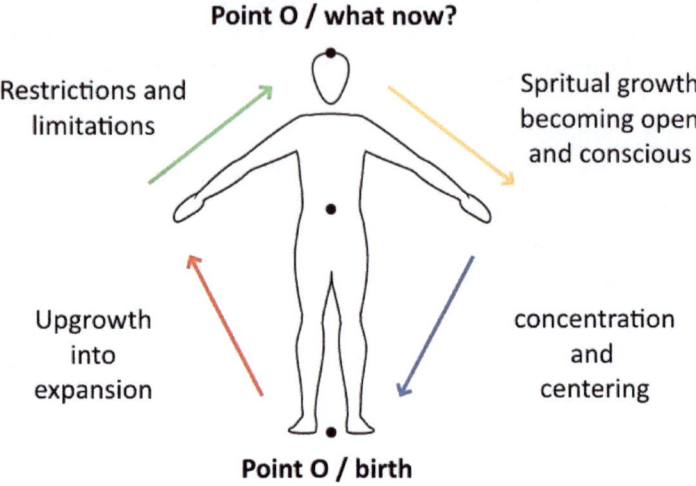

With the help of this drawing, you can see how you ascend from point 0, your birth, to an adult. By expanding into the pole of matter and the splitting of yourself, you separate yourself from your original unit. You now are grown-up and tall, but inside, you feel small and lost in relation to the massive pole of matter. The outside that you have created yourself is overpowering and restricting you. You then arrive at point 0 by asking you: what now. Your inner Self is pushing you to a change. You start to ask yourself why you live – what purpose lies behind the matter. By searching for answers, you begin to concentrate more on yourself and are ready to deal with yourself and your life. Your new way is: **To find back to your wholeness and to become aware of being the center of all that is.**

By stepping into the spiritual path, you will scrutinize all your 'I have to's and I musts' as these are your wrong doctrines and thought patterns that you have stored inside for a long time.

Consequently, you will be able
- To take on responsibility for yourself
- To critically look at situations you are experiencing
- To love you yourself
- To believe in yourself
- To use your fire and your energy for yourself and your growth
- To understand yourself
- To open up for your inner voice
- To have faith in yourself
- To be aware that only you yourself can truly help you
- To take the initiative for changes
- To stop suffering and having feelings of guilt
- To stop accusing the outside but to learn to see your own mistakes mirrored by your friends
- To start to live
- To find self-fulfillment and your potential capacities

On this path to your inner world, you will become conscious that all there is in the outside is part of yourself! As a surgeon, you will be able to cut away ulcers (old doctrines and thought-patterns) that have constrained you in the past. As scientists, you seek new experiences that will bring you more wisdom and finally expanded knowledge. As a lawyer, you see the principals of coherence and thereby enlighten the matters of fact to judge a situation yourself. At the same time, you are an architect drawing designs for the future that your inner engineer and foreman put into the matter.

You often imagine how this or that could be. But your wishes hardly ever materialize as you do not believe in your power and capability of creating your reality. It is your constricted and limited ideas that let the wonders not come through. You yourself stand in your way. Artistic people around you mirror your ability to creating new things – you are the creator – creating from moment to moment a new unique situation!

Your chosen path through matter is:
After having stepped out of your wholeness, the 0, you are walking into the complete separation from yourself, feeling lost. By becoming conscious, you will finally return to your center, the unit from where you came and what you are!

Becoming conscious

Without a fundamental change of your opinions and your actions, you will be captured in the treadmill of life further on. You have to seek out all of your restricting beliefs, thought- and behavior-patterns, get aware of them, and subsequently release them to change yourself and your reality. You are energetic and capable of doing so and thus will live accordingly to your inner needs. Let your inner fire and urge guide you to reach expansion! Open the barriers and search for your secret wishes and desires. Become honest with yourself and take over personal responsibility! Become aware that you are the center of your subjective perceived reality. Wake up! Realize the reasons why you, out of your inner unconscious side, realize this or that in life!

Don't forget that your spirit makes the matter. Therefore find the causes of what you experience in yourself! Begin to check who and what rejects you into your old behavior and stop calling or seeing these people as they are past projections of yourself who you do not need on your new path anymore. As long as you hold on to your 'old' programs, you stay in the imprisonment of the blockades that you built up yourself a long time ago. Start now to dare to let go from your past structures and live – move forward!

Take your apartment as an example. You all know the problem: over the years, you endlessly have collected things and cannot throw them away. Your desire to get more finally makes you lose free space or 'your breath'. Then comes the moment you get aware that you have to change something, let go of old things to have room for the new. When you do not act voluntarily, you will be forced by the outer circumstances, the so-called fate. The fact yet is that it always is your 'inner baby', your center, that cries for changes and ameliorations. It materializes these essential changes in your life for you to become agile again. You yourself are responsible for your life! You are capable of realizing which old patterns are hemming you. And you alone can change yourself and become open to the exciting experiences ahead!

The first step to understand your multidimensional being is gaining clarity on the here and now. Do not forget that you are the maker of matter. All there is in the mirror of the outside is part of yourself! Learn to view people, situations, and circumstances from another angle and begin to translate them as part of yourself. Become aware of what they want to tell you – what the inner Self wants to teach you or where it wants you to change.

Everything that happens makes sense. And everything that you experience is related to you. It is your own reality and always is right for your advancement! Knowing this, you will be able to see the positive side in every situation, although it seems 'negative' first. Out of the negative, you become active and open for further experiences to grow and increase your knowledge. You will reach the point of accepting your life fully. By being able to do so, you will not denounce anything nor divide yourself anymore but will see the positive in all that is – this saying YES is true love!

Being aware that you are the creator of your mirrored reality and the center of all, you have to understand that you have to love and respect yourself first. Only then will you be able to 'love' the outside you create in each moment. Altruism, as you know from the past, usually has to do with the sacrifice of yourself. You were searching for love, buying love, and in doing so, forgot yourself or even gave yourself up. You have to change this attitude! When you love yourself, you beam this love out, and it will stream back to you from various parts of the world.

Realize your power and become conscious that you are not a puppet on the string dancing along with the will of somebody but the center, the main character in your self-created theatre. When you change, you will become aware of how the outside is changing accordingly. You will enjoy the positive echoes streaming back to you!

When I started my way into becoming aware of reality, I read a book about how to love yourself. I learned to embrace myself, to accept myself. I cannot remember whether it was my idea, but I anyway supported myself by writing with red lipstick on the mirror in my bathroom: I love myself – I am 'good' – I stand up to myself! We usually look into the mirror before we go to bed as well as in the morning when we wake up. By writing positive sentences over our reflection, we augment the belief in ourselves. Many of my friends have copied this idea, and the results always were fascinating. We all felt much better and stronger. We learned to say no to people or situations drawing us back into old patterns and yes to new challenges and exciting persons.

The principle of polarity

Initially watches only show 12 hours of a day and not the whole 24 hours. 0.00, 12.00, and 24.00 o'clock are at the same point. The 2 poles of light and dark, day and night, are not separated but melt into each other.

If you design a clock with 2 circles including the 24 hours you get an 8 that shows the polarity:

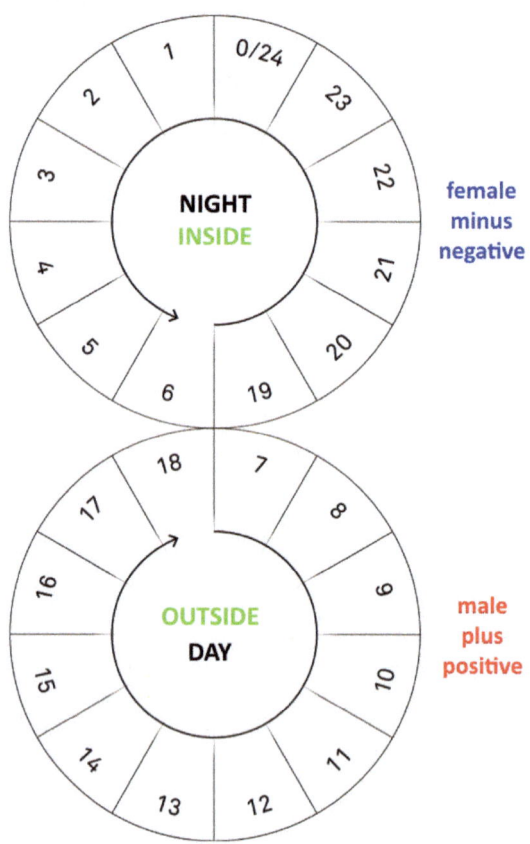

In this drawing of the time, the upper female, negative circle turns backwardly, whereas the lower male, the positive circle, forwardly turns around. And yet, time always moves on. Backward and forward complement each other and become one together. This movement explains that the female and the male pole always fuse. Only together, they realize the dissolution of the old and the creation of the new.

After having passed the night, you start your day entering the male pole at 6.00 am. You separate yourself from the dark, the unconsciousness where your reality created. During the day, you dance in your self-constructed 'theatre' from where you withdraw yourself to your inner world in the evening to spiritually create your next day overnight.

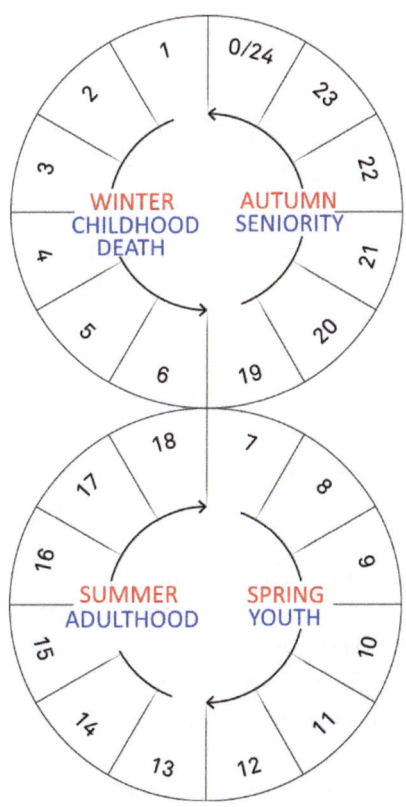

The circle of one day corresponds with the one of a year: From 6.00 to 12.00 equals spring when nature starts to sprout and to enfold. From 12.00 to 18.00 in the summertime, the sun brings warmth and lets the fruits become ripe. 18.00 to 24.00 equals autumn when the trees lose their leaves and withdraw their energy into the inside. And from 24.00 or 0.00 until 6.00 is wintertime when the new is developing in the shelter of the dark until it shows up in spring.

The same procedure applies to your life. In your childhood from 0.00 to 6.00, you are 'hatched' and taken care of your parents. At this age, you are still natural and free of morals and rationality. Your fantasies are infinite. Slowly you are learning to believe in the matter that you create yourself and to be fascinated by the outside. By then, you begin to give this outside more importance than to yourself and consequently have to obey.

6.00 to 12.00 equals spring – your youth. You go out into the pole of matter. Now you must deal with the world, have to learn what is right and wrong, and have to take over first responsibilities. You separate the 'I' from the YOU what makes you insecure. Therefore you often have to defend yourself. On the other side, you start to be attracted by the YOU's searching for your second half, the ideal partner, and hoping to become happy with him. This springtime is the preparation for your next step into adulthood by learning to be independent.

12.00 to 18.00 stands for the age of maturity and consolidation. You have grown up and start to become entrenched in the matter. You also are creating by having children and tangible assets. You augment your magnitude in the outside. Now you believe in the power and validity of matter; you center your thinking and acting on rationality and moral regulations. You are not conscious of the truth that you are creating all that is yourself. Therefore you fight against threads and try to secure yourself and your belongings. Being completely separated from your inner center, you believe in living, although you undermine your real needs and wishes out of consideration for the outside.

18.00 to 24.00/0.00 is the time of aging. You retire from working and thus finally find time and leisure to concentrate on yourself and retrospect your past. Your acting becomes slower and less oriented to the outside. By doing so, you change your attitudes and are now open to the spiritual world inside you.

The time from 0.00 to 6.00 is the phase of death that parallelly stands for childhood again. During this time, the old dissolves, and the 'new' is starting to crystallize. As New Year's Eve – the past year gives way and flows into the coming one. In matter, everything always results from the other.

Death as the antipole to life corresponds with your sleep, your unconsciousness. By letting go of yesterday, you spiritually create your life and reality of the next day during the night. Your subjectively perceived reality is the result of your thoughts and your beliefs that you take into your sleep accompanied with your inner fire and urge for enhancement. Thus death means the dissolution of the old as well as bringing forth the new. Therefore do not hold onto structures that suppress and constrain your movement anymore. Say yes to the death of the past! Free yourself of the one-sided and monopolar perspective and win back your original truth, the holistic view by becoming conscious.

It is fascinating that 0, 12, and 24 show the birthdate of Jesus Christ: 24.12.0000 – this date symbolizes your path through the pole of matter, starting at the 0 with your birth. Then the having to separate from your inner Self into the other pole to the 12 and subsequently turning back to your origin at the $24 = 0$.

By becoming aware, you will be able to combine these 2 poles of death and life, spirit and matter, and me and you. You will then merge your outside with your inside, the darkness with the light, and thus achieve clear-sightedness and wholeness again.

The YOU is reflecting the darkness to enlighten your 'I'.

Every single 'YOU' as well as your subjectively perceived reality mirror the dark and the unconscious parts of yourself. What is hidden inside is reflected in your outside! The moment you start not fighting off but facing up with the 'YOU's' around you, you will get to know the multidimensional 'I' as all there is is part of yourself.

Your fellows are playing roles in your self created theatre. They are mirrors of yourself and help you to enlighten your thought- and behavior-patterns. When you observe faults in your fellows, you will, when you look closely, find out that they reflect your own wrong mistakes. Whatever you criticize or 'sermonize' concerns yourself. Are you envying somebody you are not aware of your own inner abundance and your value. And when a 'YOU', an aspect of yourself disappears from your field of vision, you have inwardly changed and do not need this projection of yourself anymore – it dissolves, and a new one will take its place in reality.

There always is a movement between 2 poles. It is in your breathing in and out as well in your blood circulation. The infow is the realizing, the becoming aware of something (the blue blood in the veins). The outflow (the red blood in the arteries) shows the realizing, the creating of the new. This movement of in and out, out and in, i.e., of your inside and your outside is **your soul**. It brings to matter and reality what is hidden in your inner world.

As long as you struggle against the outside, you are not in tune with yourself – you separate your inner Self from the projection outside – your soul is divided. The time has come to start combining your 2 poles, the inside, and the outside! You only can achieve harmony with yourself when you become conscious of this movement, this flow. Out of what you realize in the evening, you realize your tomorrow – the inflow that you take into your sleep is flowing out into your reality the next morning! If you want to change your reality and your life, you must start enlightening your inside by understanding the theater in your outside before you go to sleep. The more you concentrate and see the grievances the faster you get aware of your thoughts, beliefs, and behavior-patterns that constrict you and can let them go. And the more you start to see the many positive things spread in your reality, the sooner you are getting aware of the wealth you carry inside yourself.

Polarity:
– the side beyond – this side
– everything – nothing
– life – death
– inside – outside
– infinity – transience
– boundlessness – limits
– unfathomable – impalpable
– now – sequences
– wealth – poverty
– joy – mourning
– white – black
– <u>unconsciousness – reflection in matter</u>

By putting your attention on the polarity, you will find the answers to why you are living and why you have chosen the path through matter. You will become aware

– that you will not die but be infinite and forever
– that you should say yes to death as it creates life
– that you are not bound in limits but have complete liberty
– that there are no boundaries, and therefore everything is possible
– that you can learn to understand your 'chaotic' spiritual origin through logic order in the matter
– that there is no succession, but that all takes place here and now
– that you only can get to know yourself and the truth behind by becoming conscious of the shiny and reflecting matter.

By going on this new path into your inner spiritual world, you will learn:

That you first had to separate yourself from your origin to become aware that **you are the center of the reality that you create yourself.**

That **you yourself materialize your reality through your thoughts, your beliefs, and behavior habits.**

That **all that you perceive in the outside is an illusion, is the mirror of your inner Self.**

That you first must deal with limits and the feeling of being nothing to **become then conscious of the stupefying spiritual 'I' who is free and has got all the possibilities to create paradise.** Do not forget that you only know what hot means when you have burned in the past. Joy only when you've been sad before.

That **you chose this way yourself!** You will be amazed at how you will be able to change everything that you want!

Reality – the outside

The reality, the thrown out inside of yourself, is nothing else than an image, a mirror, a 'theatre', and a world full of symbols. It gives you indications and tools for you to become aware of your inner world and of the logical correlations why this or that happens in your life. You yourself are creating your own reality to get consciousness. You have 'packaged' your original wisdom in sounds and pictures to find out about your wholeness.

As an example, take the image of a tree. The tree only has stability when it is deep-rooted. You also can only reach height and expansion when you firmly stand on the ground with your 2 feet. The wind or translated the challenges that you encounter will thus not blow you away. The tree is searching for the groundwater with its roots. The same goes for you: You also must dig into your inner wisdom to grow spiritually and to unfold. Trees are being felled. Their wood makes tables, chairs, or heat when burned. This process is transformation. Be aware that by using your own fire, your will, you can achieve this same conversion of your reality.

Take the car as another example. It is a vehicle as your body. Under the bonnet lies the power that allows movement. The inside is important, not the chassis. The outside only is the paneling to protect the inside. The moment you know about your inner power, there is nothing that will slow down you anymore – you can accelerate your growth and your coming forward. You will not burn your energy for others anymore but yourself. Watch out when you get problems with your car and ask yourself where and what is hindering you from going forward.

On the contrary, you ride on the train. Your liberty to stop or turn is limited, although the train brings you to your desired destination. You do not have to interfere but can settle and carried along. Outwardly, the train reflects the masculine principle, while you give yourself over according to the feminine principle. The more you have achieved confidence in yourself, the merrier you can let your inner Self guide you instead of you struggling through situations with your head.

Here is a corresponding story I experienced years ago. From a friend of mine, I received a book I somehow rejected. After having started to read it, I woke up with the same dream on three following mornings: I was at a railway station, a train was leaving, and I just made it to get on. When the train started moving, I recognized that it was going in the wrong direction, which made me jump out at once. By questioning myself what this dream wanted to tell me, I received the answer from my inside warning me that this friend was holding me back from my new path of life. I decided not to call her anymore, which made her fade away. In succession, I met new interesting people who shared my goals.

Birds and airplanes are symbols as well: You can take off like them and thus get a broader overview. A bird turning its rounds over a forest views the forest as a whole extent. When you walk through a forest, you are concentrated on the ground to evade stumbling – you miss the overview. On the contrary, when you are looking to the sky, searching for luck in heaven, your life seems dull, and you fall over impediments you have created with your thoughts and believing patterns yourself. Start to be more attentive and to search for the reasons behind the matter. With an overview, you bring more light into the darkness, in your unconscious inside.

The theatre is a beautiful example. You see the stage with communicating actors in different scenes. Sitting in a theatre, you know that the performance is not real but fictitious. The actors are playing their part and using the words that they have memorized before.

The theatre or a movie mirrors your circle, your movement. The mentally producing author corresponds to the winter or your sleep. On the other side, you see the performance on the stage, which stands for the summer, the outside. In between, there is the director who is bringing the author's script to the stage, symbolizing spring or the morning when you organize your day. Opposite there is the audience: autumn or evening. Only when the spectator deals with the play by concentrating on becoming aware of what the author wanted to say he will understand the message that the author had put on paper.

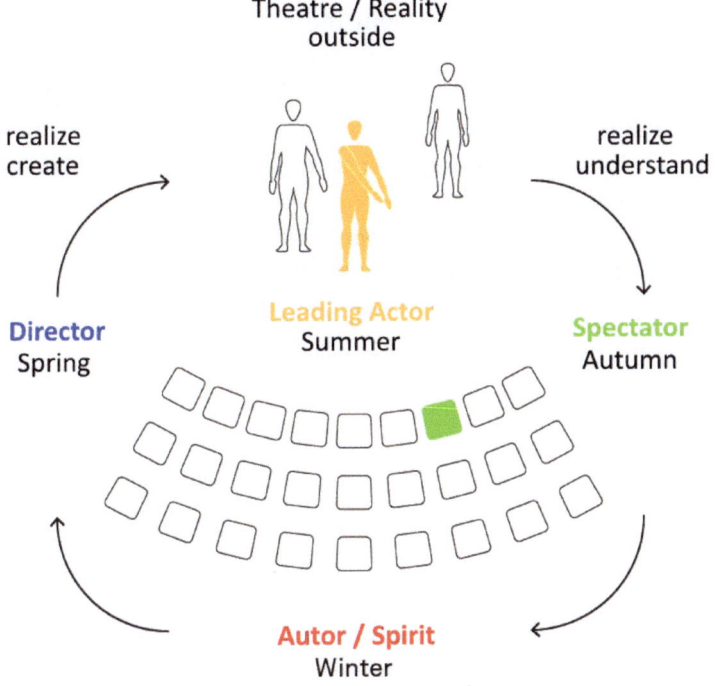

In your own theatre, you are the author, the director, and the main character in one. You are all. During your sleep, you are the author who is taking in the experiences of the day and subsequently writes the script for the next morning. Getting up, you become the director by organizing your day. In the following hours, you are the main character that you never should forget! To become aware of the background of the theatre you created yourself, **you will have to act as the spectator as well** and think about your own role as the main character. Your fellow men in your daily life are the players around you who enlighten your inner sides by communicating with you. Do not let the 'YOU' overrule you anymore but become conscious that you always are the central person around whom the whole outside is turning around!

The moment you look at your individually perceived reality from the other pole, from the standpoint of the spectator, you will realize, comprehend what lies hidden in your dark and unconscious inner Self as the outside is the mirror of your inner world. You are the author and creator of your theater, of your reality, and you have the power to change your script to the best for you. You will recognize your limiting thoughts, beliefs, and behavior structures and can reverse them into the positive side.

Unipolar one-sidedness

The concentration on the 'YOU' and the belief of the validity of matter, the other pole of your real being, make you one-sided. You build up opinions as you only regard the outside, forgetting that there always is the other pole like the coin having 2 sides. You judge many situations without hearing or seeing the other side and often condemn them as your discernment is clouded. By thinking and acting in this manner, you divide your outside from your inside and, therefore, you yourself: You are a split personality and are not the primordial 'I' anymore. You believe in the power of the outside and are not aware that the power comes from within yourself and that you yourself have all the possibilities to change what you want. With your poor-spirited beliefs, you feel small and insecure what makes you guard you against evil. You also search your luck on the outside and put all the blames away from yourself. BUT the outside is the reflection of your inner side and mirrors the meshes and entanglements you have created yourself that entangle you and thus make you being frightened. You feel cornered, and as a result, you fight – a fight against yourself. As long as you believe in the validity of the outside, you will never gain security and freedom. You will, again and again, be attacked by 'YOU's, will go on defending yourself and the things you believe to own and want to guard what is precious. At the same time, you have to abstain from so many things and your heartfully wishes. Your inside and outside are divided. Your goal is to become whole again and combine your 2 sides by raising yourself over polarity and the opposites and melt them. Subsequently, all will be as well as the other: above will become under, white as black, inside as outside. The unconsciousness becomes conscious!

Although you might have rejected egoists in your former thinking, knowing that you are the center, you have to learn to become 'egotistic' and egocentric now. It is your dark side in yourself against that you have been fighting. Accepting your ego that creates all that is, you will realize that if you yourself are feeling well, consequently your co-players in your theatre feel better as well. You are the origin of everything that flows back to you from your reality, as everything is part of yourself. The moment you change your beliefs and watch at the outside from a different angle, you can act differently and perceive the new echoes. Some 'old' friends might fade away because you are not playing your old role anymore, but there will be enough new people who will support you on your 'new' path.

You might have disguised or having worn a mask once in your life and remember how freely and unforced you felt playing another role. At such times you forget your daily routine and your 'normal' role-playing – you live in an altered 'world' and dare to go up to foreign 'YOU's' freely talking to them. An original part of yourself is manifesting itself as a child in such situations. Why should this incredible naive openness be suppressed any longer by your believes and behavior patterns? Become aware of what is restricting you and change your attitude, your programs!

Mirror of yourself

You can only get a momentary physical picture of yourself by a look in the mirror. The same happens when you want to know what is inside you – what you see on the outside, in your reality, is the mirror of your inside. You are in the center! You have created everything that happens. Realize that it is you who is responsible for your reflected theatre by realizing what you should change to become happy.

Did you ever think about the fact that you never see your face as all the others do? In the mirror, you get a reversed image. Your left side is where the 'YOU's' have their right side. If you want to see you 'correctly', you have to have a picture or a video taken. But these always lay in the past. Your expression at that moment is not now. Really 'seeing' you yourself here and now only is possible when you watch the people around you as mirrored projections of yourself – parts or aspects of your magnificent 'I'.

The YOU mirrors the darkness to enlighten your I!

And remember that you split your entity into all that you perceive. Thus everything that you see and hear is part of yourself. Nature, the weather, animals, and mainly the people with who you directly communicate are materialized aspects of your 'I' at that moment. Viewed in this light, a dialog with a 'YOU' is monolog with your inner Self. By interchange, your fellow human beings help you to pronounce your thoughts into words – bring them out, accentuating with sound what intensifies them. The words you hear are the echoes of your subconsciousness as well and therefore help you to enlighten your thoughts and beliefs. By paying attention to the stories of the 'YOU's', you can find out from what old structures you should free yourself. Without knowing the 'old' programs that guide you and reprograming them, your life won't change!

Surely you have already noticed that certain people get into similar situations again and again. Often they change their partners, their job, because they are poorly treated, are not respected, and hope to find a better life afterward. Because they do not look for the causes in themselves, the next relationship, the next job with small nuances, brings them back into the same situation, from which they must free themselves again. Without knowledge of one's own stored programs, which have to be changed, there are no fundamental changes in life!

It is essential to see the positive sides of your co-players as well. Be happy about all the cheerful and encouraging echoes – might it be a person, a child, an animal, or the sun that sheds its radiance toward you. This view is most important in times when you are feeling down as just a little smile shows you your positive inner side.

When you change your attitude, you will perceive these changes and your new looking at reality echoed by the persons or animals around you. Some of your aspects of yourself will fade away. Although having enjoyed their company for a long time, they suddenly or slowly go away from you. You might scrutinize yourself why you do not see them anymore. The reason is that when you inwardly change, you do not need these aspects of yourself any longer – you yourself de-materialize them. Letting them go makes you free to experience new perspectives and new beings. Real living means moving! Therefore changes are necessary. Acknowledge that it is you yourself that creates the reality and therefore be not sad when some of your close relations say good-bye. The holes that they leave behind will fill with new aspects of yourself with who you will mentally grow.

Death

In nature, there always follows something new when the old dies. The leaves fall to the ground in autumn because the tree pulls its energies inside to produce fresh leaves in spring again. The validity of the old is over and brings out the new. Only by letting go from and disposing of the old the new can enfold.

You already might have had to deal with death while having lost a precious being, a person, or an animal. You usually do not understand the reason behind: It is your own inner will to go forward that brings you the changes as an old routine has lost its validity.

Death wants to teach you that you should never stick to routines and too old structures. Your inside intends to move, to live, and to go through new experiences. The word pass has different meanings – passing away means dying, whereas the pass indicates the movement to go from one side to another, be it in the mountains or when you pass your final exams. Going forward in your life, you have to let the old dye.

The farewell of a partner, friend, or sometimes an article always mirrors your inner will to move. Old thoughts and believes fade away and are being replaced with new impressions and pictures in your reality. Do not be sad anymore or hang on to your past but live in the here and now. Be aware who is pulling you back into your old patterns and free yourself by being open for your new fellow beings. Life means movement, and transformation.

When I was young, I saw a theatre where the stage was rotating after a specific time of the performance. I cannot remember the title but remember very well that the main character left the old side and the co-players behind by going through a door and stepping into the new side of the stage to go on playing his role with new actors.

This passing through a door made a big impression on me and explained to me the picture of somebody dying. The bereaved mourn and mostly think about what they miss or what they should have done before. When we live our life without regrets, we will always be able to let the 'old' that had validity yesterday go today. Whenever I meet mourning people, I tell them this story and advise them to send out thoughts of strength to themselves and to the aspect that has gone for the passage into another experience.

Thoughts, beliefs, and behavior patterns

As long as you believe in the validity of matter, your going forward will always be limited. These constraints you built up by your convictions yourself some time ago will be shown to you again and again. Yet only by checking them, you can learn to change your attitude and free yourself from your limiting thoughts. And to build up new beliefs of being able to achieve a happy life.

Spirit is free, limitless, and eternal. When you were young, you took over the beliefs of fears, restrictions, finiteness, conventions, and rules from your parents and saved them as programs. The adults told you that a table or a wall is hard. They also told you that you would be sick when you walk around with wet hair, and as you believed what they were telling you – you became ill. In your lifetime, you are encountering a lot of such warnings that you save and think that they are the reality. Therefore you have built up your thought- and belief-patterns.

Yet you are the maker of your own reality – it is the mirror of what you think and believe. All there is in the outside is the pictured reflection of your inside. Take as an example the fact of seeing everywhere the car you just decided to buy. Or being pregnant, you manifest other pregnant women. Even using a new word will suddenly make you hear it around you.

The thoughts that you put into sound, into words have the power to materialize in your reality. As long as you apprehend the worst and speak out your fears, you will live through situations that will confront you with them. And when you are full of negativity and criticize everything, you will have to undergo unpleasant happenings. You are not aware of being able to change this by concentrating on the positive sides of your life. But you can by using your fire and courage!

Do not discuss your problems with your 'old' friends over and over again and put desperate thoughts into your words. Begin to be open to somebody who can objectively look at the situation from further away. He/she will help you to get a different view of the situation – look at the other pole of the coin. By doing this, you will learn not to put the problem in the outside but search the root cause in yourself, in your thoughts and your behavior patterns. How often has it happened that by wallowing problems you lost the overview, for the trees you couldn't see the forest anymore. In such situations, you stand and turn in place and mentally pull yourself down. Move for- and up-ward by finding the solutions in yourself!

How many people do you know who try to get a better image through clothes, jewelry, or cars? By acting like this, they believe to please the outside and to be rated higher. Please has two meanings: to satisfy and to ask for something. By wanting to please the outside, you always are begging for a sweet response as you yourself are not self-secure and thus are making yourself small. To overplay this deficiency of worth, people 'decorate' themselves with material values.

If you want to become 'strong' and valuable, you have to change your attitude. Start to look at your life and your daily situations from a distance – you will then find out what hides in yourself. Look at yourself in the mirror and ask yourself if the actual hairdo is suiting you. Can it be that your husband likes it or that you adapted it because it is 'in' at the moment? Do you wear clothes that might not fit you because you never took a look from the back? Do you eat meals or spices you do not digest just to please the others? Or do you meet people with who you are not amused, just because of your children or your husband? As long as you adapt yourself to rules emitted by the others, you will not live!

You will go on materializing unhappy situations again and again as long as you hang on to your old belief that the outside has more power than you. And as long as you behave the same way, again and again, your reality will not change. Become aware that you are the creator of your reality and start to be honest with yourself! Stand up and trust in yourself!

These words reminded me of the time when I was married. My hair had become thin through permanent waves and almost blond through strands. The mirror showed a stranger because I had lost myself. One day I made a decision and went to an American hairdressing salon in Munich. In the morning, my husband for whom I had changed my hairdo warned me not to come back with my original dark brown hair and a short hairstyle – I came home changed with exactly this hairdo – self-secure and happy for having found back to myself again. After 4 months, I was ready to say good-bye to him and subsequently got divorced.

Take yourself in your arms and accept yourself as you are! Why should you not trust in yourself? Why should all the others be happy and not you as well? Why do you go on undermining your wishes and only wanting to fulfill the ones from other people? Why do you waste your precious energy on the others? Why do you feel empty and lost sometimes? There are many other questions – start to ask yourself for the reasons why you think you have to act like this. You will then find out about your restricted thoughts and beliefs. Being conscious of them, you can change them! **You are the center around which everything is circling!** As everything is reflecting your inside, you will get positive echoes when you change your attitudes and become happy. Your aspects, the people who will accompany you in the future, also will be happy as a result. Realizing that you realize your reality yourself and thus acting in a new way makes you strong and self-secure and effects the changes in your life!

All is always here and now – your 'original' knowledge and your inner abundance are mirrored in your reality. At the beginning of your changing your attitude, it is not possible to see the whole. Like reading a book page by page you will capture the meaning of the story only at the end. The same happens on your new path: You will understand more and more by living through experiences in your life to finally understand the wholeness. Step by step, there will be new open doors on your way of transformation. By realizing that everything is part of yourself, you will find tools and tips encouraging you. The only thing that nothing and nobody can do for you is to ask the question of WHY am I experience this or that. It is your own responsibility to find out what your inner baby wants you to change. Through materialized situations, you can become conscious of what you have to let go freeing yourself from old beliefs and behavior patterns, and act differently! You have the power to get rid of the old limitations and thus become free and open for the new! You can compare this to getting a new house. Before you can build it, you have to pull the old one down and make a stable fundament. You have to rip down the old that has no validity anymore and translated fill the hole with new and forward bringing thoughts and actions. Your newly won self-confidence and your positive attitude will change yourself and your life. And every altered activity and all your positive words will be saved as new programs in your computer, in your inner side.

Here is a story of mine: For a long time, I went walking the dogs with a lady who was negative, very possessive, and was telling me of her problems all the time. The walks were not pleasant and I mostly got back home in a sad mood. Even the dogs became aggressive towards other dogs we met. My inner voice started to warn me that I should quit this routine and stop seeing her. But I did not dare to make the break. Shortly after, my knee began to hurt, which told me that something was wrong with my movement. When I played the Tarot cards, which at that time often gave me the answers, I picked: Laziness. The text was saying that I had to learn to distance myself from situations I did not like and to say no. I got the message again, changed my walks, and the lady faded away. Out of this story, I learned that the new thinking has to settle first before we can easily put it into action. We must train ourselves over and over again until the new programs work automatically and bring success and happiness all the time.

If you experience situations again and again in which you are not well, you must recognize your inner desire for movement, for a change. Put yourself in the role of the spectator in your theatre and remember that at the same time, you are the director who will materialize such situations until you as the author and the director reprogram your play, your 'I'. Experiences, actions, and positive words will subsequently save these new programs. As confirmation, the audience will applaud you for having made the necessary alternations and for making the spectacle interesting and exciting.

It is very important that you do not only concentrate on the 'bad' situations but start to see the many positive things in your life. Look up into the sky and watch the funny clouds moving. Or go for a walk in nature – all the beauty you see is the mirror of your inside! There you can comprehend that the seeds planted in the earth in autumn are developing during winter to become strong and willing to show up in springtime. The same happens with you – the thoughts you take into your sleep will materialize the next morning. Whenever you go to bed with too much new information and cannot bring them into a meaningful understanding, you will wake up the following day with a headache. In your old thinking, you will blame the alcohol or too many cigarettes for the rotating head. But it is you yourself who has not reflected on the many inputs of the evening before having let the information float away by not being attentive. Or you will experience that you will be sick in the morning because you took the thought, someone infected me with a disease, into your sleep.

Therefore go to bed every night with a smile on your face and in your heart. Concentrate yourself on the many positive things you have experienced during the day. The result is that you create a better reality at night and will look at it more positively day by day. And in case you wake up at night with problems whirling in circles, and you cannot free yourself of this pulling down spiral, get up and stop it by taking a piece of paper and write down the positive memories. Being in a positive mood makes you see the problem lighter, it can even be solved by itself. Remember: There is no time – the solution of a problem thus already is right at the beginning.

At the time I had the idea to write a diary before I went to bed. In this book, I allowed myself only to put positive experiences. In the beginning, this was a hard task as I caught myself having so many negatively poled views of my reality. Did I have only 2 lines in my book, in the beginning, I became better already after a week. My inner will to see and hear more positive things during the day to fill my pages changed my attitude. Or let it put it this way: I materialized more and more that was joyful and echoing my inner happiness. All these friends of mine who were eager to alter and become more conscious followed my advice and made a lot of beautiful jumps in their future life. Some others liked the idea, but they did not find the time…

Every 'you' is free to do, or to let it be but: Everybody is the architect of his own fortune – the author of his own theatre!

The Word

'And the earth was desolate and empty, and it was dark on the deep, and the Spirit of God floated on the water. And God said, let there be light. And there was light.'

The spirit manifests itself through the WORD.

The word out of which the world has become – is 'wor(l)ded'!

The word has power! With words, the language condenses and centers your thoughts, accentuates them, 'prints them out' and throws them into the outside, from where they echo.

In the restaurant, you have a menu in front of you. You choose from the written texts, the meal, and the drink that you want. You express your wishes in words that will soon materialize without you being aware of the work in the background of the kitchen. Or you drive into town and need a parking space. Speak the positive sentence: Of course, I find a free place, then you find it.

But how little are you aware of what you're saying? How can you ever be slim if, every day, you put the opponent into words: I am too fat? How can you be rich or become wealthy if you keep telling yourself and others that you would like to have this or that, but have too little money? How can your mirror image make you happy if you're always upset about small blemishes? Why do you respond to a compliment, the dress looks very nice on you, with oh, it's old, instead of just saying thank you.

Become aware of the 'outflow', how and what you pronounce, and the consequences. Think again about your blood circulation. If the red flow from your heart into your body is full of poison, full of negativity, then the body reports back that is sick and weak – you are getting sick. So think first before you speak and choose only those words that are positive for you and others. The positive will come back to you like a smile as an echo.

The following experience taught me a lot. A friend of mine had a small house with three floors close to Lugano, the central city in the South of Switzerland. At the top was the bedroom with a window front from the floor to the ceiling. I spoke out my fears; one of my dogs could fall. Although we took precautions in the form of a stretched net, it still happened. During a thunderstorm, the male dog fell – not out of the window, but down the steep steps inside, and lay there with a dislocated joint. My fears, expressed in words, had materialized. It was an awful experience for me, and I was glad that I could reposition the joint myself. From then on, I have been paying very close attention to what I say, immediately breaking off a sentence with negative polarity and altering it into a positive one.

You sometimes listen to a person, are 'in bondage' to him, because you believe in the 'YOU', in the outside. Be aware that when you give power to the 'YOU', the words of the 'YOU' also have the 'power' to manifest. They are always your own thoughts that are echoing back to you, are your learned belief patterns stored on your 'hard disk' as: If you do this or that, then you become ill. When you eat a lot, you get fat. If you learn nothing, you become nothing. If you drink too much, you get stupid and so on. You yourselves believe in these words, so they materialize.

When you lament your fate, you accuse yourself and fall into self-pity because you suffer. Consider that pity also means lamentation and regret. But you are not born to regret nor to suffer. You are materializing this earthly existence to live and enjoy in the here and now! There is no fate, no guilt of others – everyone is solely responsible; everyone creates his own reality. Therefore begin to become aware of what you are putting into words. Concentrate on saying what is 'good' and beautiful instead of emphasizing what is all wrong – poisoning you and your life. Positive words illuminate your reality.

When I began to speak out positive words, I noticed that negative thoughts still were noticeable in the background. When I answered the question of a friend: 'How are you?' with: I'm fine, it shouted in me: Actually, I'm not doing well. I then learned to 'shoot down' these old destructive 'poison dwarves' with a loud 'no'. I started to tell myself that I had had so much luck so far and will continue to have it. This change of recognizing and acting differently from then on brought more and more beautiful things into my life. Today I know that I am happy because I realize happiness myself and that it therefore, comes back to me like an echo.

The word is of enormous importance! The word is a sound and a wave. If you throw a stone into a lake, you will see circular waves, some of which come back to you. What you let flow out of your inner being comes back to you like a response from outside. It is the 'answer', the echo, the 'anti-word'. At the same time, the waves go in all directions. So if you change your choice of words, it will flow out in all directions and cause the change of your reality.

The spoken word causes a movement and corresponds to a flowing, but it is also printed on paper. Hence, 'influence' and 'impression'. You assume that the outside influences or impresses you. This is not the case. You yourselves are the authors, the creators of your reality. With your spoken or written word, you decide your life. You are responsible for your own words and answers! Become aware of the deeper meaning behind everything and change your views and statements to enjoy the answers.

The word also makes statements. Status means position, state, or place where you are. By words, you declare your stand-point, but you can locate, discover yourself as well by understanding the logical connections with your state of mind.

You can also become conscious through stories of fellow men that are echoes of your inner voice. You were used to listening to them and quickly ready to advise the other person. Recognize that what you hear is like a chapter in your own book, illuminating your own current situation. And your answers to the 'YOU's always are in fact messages to yourself – you are making conversation with your inner voice!

Self-recognition aids

All the tools like cards, astrology, numerology, runes, Bach Flowers, and many more you have 'created' yourself to 'tell the truth'. Fortune-telling is often associated with predicting the future. This is not true because you only learn the truth about your current thinking and beliefs. You create the new from the now. Forecasting the future is problematic because you are sticking to something that may happen at some point. You expect, that is, you wait for things and situations, whether they be good or bad, and you are not open to change. You build up a belief through a prognosis, from which you are waiting for the confirmation manifesting in reality.

If my friends and I lay cards, become aware of their statements, and put them again minutes later, another statement results – we recognize the problems in the conversation and develop ideas for a change. Through the cards, we grasp the here and now, we change by becoming aware of our belief and behavior patterns and therefore create a different echo immediately afterward.

All tools, as well as people, animals, situations, diseases, even a film on television or a book, you materialize to see your true Self from a different perspective, to get to know it and thereby change your views and prejudices.

What you experience, look at, or hear leads you to ever more profound insights about yourself. The outside is the fragmentation and division of your Self into countless beings, images, and symbols. But you are always in the center and have your subjective perception. So stay with yourself and concentrate on what is happening to you. Become aware of your responsibility to yourself!

You will begin to see and hear in other ways. You will learn to 'translate' situations and to convert the central themes from the play you are experiencing, on you, and relate them to yourself. You then step into a new way of thinking and a new dimension of consciousness. No longer to accept what is as such, but to realize how you can change it, 'realize' it differently. Open yourselves to the inner, the hidden, and you will find that you are becoming permeable to your inner voice and your inspirations. This will give you security and confidence in your perception, and reality will become more apparent and more transparent. The more you focus on it, the faster you can free yourself from the entanglements and shackles and change yourself and your life.

Change is movement. The blood – your elixir of life reflects this flow from out, in, and vice versa from in, out – from <u>realization and realization</u>. In this world, where this movement manifests itself, among other things through time, one always follows the other. This is your experience in polarity. So the more you grasp the flow between your 'I' and the whole, between your inner and outer, the more you recognize your own barriers and can break them with a smile. By concentrating on the moment, your thoughts, words, and consciousness become more precise and more positive. Everything that is you will eventually be able to center on a single point, the 0.

The centering on yourself corresponds to the black, the core, and thus the concentrated energy. This symbolism you find in targets or the so-called black holes. In former times it was assumed that UFOs (Unidentified Flying Objects) 'slip' through such black holes into our galaxy and materialize here. You also create the image of the UFO yourself to become aware that you can think in other dimensions and to rise above time and space.

When I began to deal with the various aids, stories of extraterrestrials fascinated me. One evening, as I was saying goodbye to a friend of mine in front of my house, with whom I had talked intensively about such stories, a light suddenly appeared in the night sky approaching us. We returned to my balcony and observed the object, which suddenly stopped. It was yellow in the middle, like a big star, and shone red at the top. At the bottom, it turned and radiated green light, like spotlights. We called the tower of Zurich Airport. At that time, this was possible. The duty manager told us that there was no airplane on the radar and that it had to be something strange, inexplicable. He told us that he often gets such calls at night, but unfortunately, he has never seen an apparition like the one described to him. After about two hours, the light rushed west at an incredible speed and disappeared.

From our concentration on the subject of extraterrestrials, this experience has materialized.

And it happened again. During a holiday in Mallorca, a friend and I sat by the sea and looked at the starry sky. I said casually: Tonight it is possible that we see a UFO ... My words materialized: A bright light like years ago appeared out of nowhere, moved towards us, and rushed away again after some time with unexplainable speed towards the west.

If you find your way back to your center, the black, then you will solve all questions and problems according to the white (I know): For black is white – matter is the spirit. Be conscious of the movement in the form of the 8, which unites inside and outside. Thus your soul is no longer divided – the flow is harmonious and full of love. You then become aware of your multidimensional 'I', your true talents, desires, and needs and begin to live them out and enjoy them. The more satisfied and happier you are, the more you acknowledge and love yourself, the more joyful and colorful your life will become. Break down your walls now so that your inner fullness can pour into reality.

So, sit down with the tools that are around you at all times, deal with them, and ask yourself:
– WHY?
– What would I like to do?
– What prevents me from doing it?
– What forces me to do things I don't want to do?

Many more questions will come to your mind.

As long as you think about what the 'YOU' probably means and says about yourself, you turn in circles. You give power to the 'YOU', search in vain for explanations or solutions, and thus get more and more into a downward spiral. You feel empty because you are wasting your energy. You put yourself behind the light – 'behind your inner sun'. You can change that!

Finally, be honest with yourself and take responsibility for yourself. It is just your stored belief that something has always been and thus must always be and that you cannot change anything. No, everything is transient and 'wonderfully' changeable!

In the following, the self-help aspects are examined. First of all, a look is taken at your own physical aids: the senses and the diseases. Thereafter you will get a look at the external 'aids', Bach flowers, tarot, astrology, etc.

The Senses

Just as you have five fingers to grasp, you have five 'material' senses to understand: seeing, hearing, smelling, tasting, and touching. With these five senses, you can perceive and then question what you see, hear, smell, taste, or feel. They are your very own tools for becoming conscious.

Someone does not have his five senses together means that such a person is confused – he does not stand by himself, has no own point of view. If someone is no longer potent of his senses, then he no longer has control over himself.

By **seeing** you perceive what you are looking at. You see images that are symbols and mirrors of your being that reflect what is important to you from different angles. Learn to unite these various images into one, just as you condense the thousands of colored moving dots, pixels, into a picture when you watch television. The image you see is the expression of what you have previously created, entered in your computer.

The computer language bases on 0 and 1, yes and no, i.e., on polarity. Equally, the whole truth, as well as the momentary consciousness of the 'I' always mirrors in pictures simultaneously. So the reflection on the outside is truth and deception. You deceive yourselves as you are not conscious of the whole. You concentrate only on individual sections of the entire and thus divide, split your Self, which means the splitting of the 'I'.

But if you look ('lug' in Swiss German means 'the lie') at the situation from another perspective, then the lie you have been living with for years dissolves, and you become aware that you 'lie' and where you lie instead of moving. You realize what you have valued and what you need to 'value' with changed consciousness anew. The more you concentrate on the 'I', and the more the 'whole' mirrored world view you put into your own hands, the more your spiritual and holistic view expands – not both as well as but homopolar, simultaneous, and equally valid.

If very young people are rather 'short-sighted', then older people who are 'more mature' and 'wiser' will show farsightedness. Young people do not think about tomorrow – they live! They are not yet aware of the dangers. It lacks maturity, an expanded vision. Far-sightedness means that you look at things from a distance to grasp the whole. But this must not tempt you of being stuck in sad or beautiful memories nor thinking about tomorrow. It means instead to live and rejoice in the here and now. Open your eyes and unite the short and the long sight!

On television, I saw an earthquake destroy parts of San Francisco years ago. What did this story want to tell me? I thought about how many people had to move and asked myself if this could affect me too. And lo and behold, without warning from the owners, three days later, my resignation fluttered into my house. Unconsciously it was me myself who realized this change, and it was mirrored to me on the outside, on TV.

Since my childhood, I thought of signs to recognize. During my school days, I was already so 'good' at it that I knew my grades in advance through red lights and other clues. So I never experienced a surprise after exams, because I already knew what to expect.

When I wanted to find a companion for my male dog I looked for 4- and 5-leaf cloverleaves as signs. Three times I deflagrated my energies because although I had not seen a positive sign, I traveled to look at dogs. Then I discovered a breed, which 'by chance', had 17 puppies as well as two 4-year-old female dogs I had wished for. My signs were positive – I found a 4-leaf clover on the question of whether this breed was the right one and a 5-leaf clover on my question whether one of the two older ones suited us. On the way to the breeding, I set myself the next sign by having the 'intuition' that my male should give a 'kiss' to the 'right' dog. The problem with the dogs I had looked at before always was that they came to me immediately, spread out on my lap, but growled when my male came close. The kiss should give me clarity which of the two should extend our life. It worked wonderfully: One of the females came on my lap, but the other who ignored me got the kiss. I became aware that in many situations, I did not have to make decisions from my head, but that my inner baby took them over for me, I could trust myself and let 'it' flow.

These stories have taught me to free myself from one-sided view and stubbornness into an idea. If we have confidence in ourselves, then we can rely on such signs. They are the echo of our inner being and allow us to open ourselves to those things, people, or situations that correspond positively to our development.

To hear, to listen – heart

Hearing makes you aware of noise and silence. People who do not hear are deaf. The dove is associated with peace. Peace means harmony and balance. You lose your balance and feel dizziness when you have problems with your ears.

The ears, like all sense organs, have to do with the connection between inside and outside. With the hearing-sense, you can grasp the echo of your thoughts, your own words and also become aware of your inner voice. Learn to listen and to hear what you are putting into words. And start to listen to your heart, to your inner Self.

Again a story: I had a new relationship, and for the first time in years after some time, I was ready to give this man the key to my home and to open my inner Self to him. It didn't last long, and I felt constantly dizzy. I sought help from vertigo experts at the university hospital who swiftly spinned me around from one side to the other, knocked on my ears to shake out the crystals, and even turned me upside down. Nothing helped.

Then I had an intuition: I was dizzying myself with the belief that my relationship could last longer. I ignored my partner's constant accusations and criticismus, and suppressed them. At the moment when I looked at this relationship closely and ended it, the 'swindle' was over!

It is interesting that in German one form of to 'hear' means to 'belong', i.e. to possess, to belong to a group. If you listen carefully, you can become aware of which people and thoughts you are 'in bondage' to, that is, who or what 'passes the tariff' on to you, who or what imposes conditions on you and makes you immature. Stop it! Learn with which beliefs you restrict and limit yourself and learn to judge what is valid for you and what is not. In this way, you strengthen your self-security and build trust in yourself and your perception. Then you can master all situations as you stand by yourself.

Bad hearing indicates that you do not want to hear your inner Self. You are separated from your center, shutting down and letting life and movement pass by. The same happens when older people who don't hear well withdraw from the conversation and miss the here and now. So, sharpen your ears and deal with the spoken word to become aware of the inner voice. Also, listen to your own words. Realize that when you advise others, it always has to do with yourself as the person opposite reflects your own point of view.

Listen to what you yourself express thoughtlessly through your own words. As already emphasized in the chapter 'The Word': Be mindful and catch yourself when you say negative things about yourself: 'I am sick', 'I am too fat', 'my hair is ugly today', etc. Every word is powerful and always imprints on your subconscious mind. Remember: The word from which the world is 'worded'. So how important is it to put positive things into words to hear a positive echo!

To smell – small

Smelling tells you whether something smells bad or smells good. If it stinks on the outside, you can ask yourself why this stinking smell comes toward you as a sign. Should you go on with your movement or stop and rethink it.

To have a good nose for something means to have instinct, intuition, an inner knowledge. You act instinctively, without weighing up, without including old empirical values. Isn't it astonishing that 'instinct' has almost 'stinks' in it?

If your nose is clogged, you pinch off your spiritual inspirations, virtually clog the lines. You are trapped in the treadmill of life and the network of your belief- and behavior- patterns. Thus you are not aware of the new impulses that 'flow' into you every day and are not open to the exciting challenges that would expand you.

I have told you the story of my permanently congested nose and how I solved the problem in the preface. After that, I still had a few times some phases in which I could not breathe at night. Every time the reason was that I let myself be taken in by a YOU or by commitments. After liberating myself from these shackles, my nose was as open as I was feeling.

Another 'memorable' (worthy of remembering) story: A friend had recommended me a fortune-teller. When she opened the door for me, a horrible stench of overcooked milk came towards me. I was already on my guard for caution. Then this lady claimed that my ascendant was the Virgin instead of the Taurus, as I knew. She stressed that I had stomach problems and even predicted stomach ulcers. At home, I contacted a friend who had taken courses in astrology, and she found out that the so-called fortune teller had confused 06:10 with 16:10 as the minute of birth. This experience convinced me how dangerous predictions can be.

If you become aware of the 'smell', you can grasp which people or situations are 'gasifying' and poisoning you or which are fragrant, benevolent, and allow you to let your Self blossom and unfold like a flower. As long as you do not smell properly, you feel small, inferior, and deficient. However, if you realize that you are good, always do everything right and are 'rich' (in experience and knowledge), then the old feeling of being small dissolves. You can reach out to every person, every part of yourself, because you are aware that everything is one and that everything is part of yourself – nature, the whole world, the entire universe. This knowledge is real wealth.

To taste – test

The sense of taste you also have for fashion, art, and your life in general. You get a taste, or you suddenly have a preference for something – it tastes 'good' to you. So the sense of taste has to do with your movement and development. Only when you try something, when you dare something, can you see whether it tastes good or not. But if you don't feel strong enough, temptations hit your stomach, and if you try too much, you digest poorly.

In 'temptation' is the search – the search for yourself. As long as you seek pleasure only in the outside, you will never find true fulfillment. You try to satisfy your desires with earthly things and judge and condemn if something is not to your liking. You have preferences; you love something more than another. You focus your attention on something special, in one direction. It happens not only for the food but for your momentary attitude from which you reject or accept something. As long as you love one and condemn the other, you are not one with yourself.

Your path to wholeness leads you from condemnation to judgment of what has real validity to you and what does not. With the sense of taste, you become aware of what you like – it doesn't matter to you whether the 'YOU' likes it or not. Don't care anymore if the others say that this or that should be accomplished or not; you must be honest with yourself. Through situations on the outside, perceive what you truly like and stand by it. Share what you want, what you like. Don't think about what others want but be mature and express your wishes.

The confrontation with the matter brings you tests with which you want to test yourself. With every successfully passed test, you take a step forward. If you pass new tests over and over again, your whole life will be a glittering celebration. Your goal is – not cramp and struggle, but celebration and indulgence – paradise on earth! But as long as you hesitate and reasonably think before you say or do something, you lose spontaneity and miss the chance, the moment. And the moment counts – not what was yesterday or what will be tomorrow, but what is now.

Connect your inside with the outside, be in harmony with yourself, and the outside will unfold harmoniously.
    Live, love and affirm yourself.

To touch

Touching happens through the skin cells, mainly through the hands. You can feel, for example, whether a surface is rough or smooth, cold or warm, stony or sandy. With the skin, you separate your inside from the outside. It gives you the necessary protection so that your center is not hurt. The thicker your armor is, the more insensitive and harder you are, both against the outside, where you 'run over' your fellow man lacking the necessary sensitivity, and also against your inside, where you suppress yourself and 'run over' your needs and desires.

You also know the keys from the piano. You touch, press keys to produce tones, melodies. The sound is a wave, a vibration. With 'sounds', with thoughts condensed into words, you form and shape matter. The moment you do not let yourselves oppress and smother by the faith in reality and in the 'YOU', you will vibrate and the melodies that come towards you as echoes flow harmoniously. You feel your pressure release, and you can surrender to the flow of inner movement. Free yourself from the external pressure and your compulsions, from separation, from severity. Do not chasten yourself and no longer punish you, but let yourself be touched, embraced, stroked, and caressed. You have the right to do so because you are 'good', unique, and valuable!

The 6th sense – the 'sense of feeling', the inner perception

On your way into the spiritual 'world', you will find that you have always used the 6th sense knowing. It is your spiritual perception: Without a material reason, you feel a place, an apartment, a person cold and unpleasant, in other places, with other people you immediately feel poodle-well. Without knowing why, you feel fear, pain, sadness or warmth, cheerfulness, enterprising spirit – you feel tired, slain or physically and mentally top fit.

This is about feeling, about becoming aware of your inner state when external events occur. In the sunshine, you usually feel well, free and relaxed, but sometimes you feel unhappy, alone, or guilty. The causes lie in your stored belief- patterns, which cause you problems until you have recognized and deleted them.

Do not confuse the 6th sense with compassion. As long as you believe in the importance of the 'YOU', you think that the 'YOU' needs something to make 'him' feel better. You try to slip into the 'YOU' to fulfill his wishes or expectations. With this posture, you are wasting your energies and are getting drained, sucked away. That helps neither you nor the 'YOU'. All the needs that you think the 'YOU' has are your own needs. Start to use your precious energy for yourself. Only by loving yourself you can pass this love on to the 'YOU' uncompromisingly.

Neither do speculations belong to the 6th sense, such as I have the feeling that it will rain. Do not forget that you are the makers of your reality. Speculation only expresses your beliefs, stored memories, fears, or hopes. You lack inner security. Your new attitude should be: 'I know, it's raining' because I materialize the rain.

With animals, you can recognize the 6th sense very well: Wild animals escape up to 24 hours before a tsunami, an earthquake, or a hurricane arrives. Your dog or cat will feel a thunderstorm hours before and will also recognize when a person is evaporating fear or a disease.

So if you find something or someone unpleasant, part with it/him and join happy and joyful new aspects of yourself!

Use your intuition, 'feel' yourself, and trust yourself!

The 7th sense

In contrast to the 6th sense, the feeling, the 'knowledge' does not come from the perception of external events, but directly from your inner Self. You have a sudden inspiration, enlightenment, a revelation. For example, you suddenly know that you must make a decision now, change something. Imagine that you have 'white' (I know in German) antennas that connect you to your innermost Self. Your inner baby leads you to where something still unknown to you is important: while surfing the Internet, you suddenly come across the website that opens up a new world for you. Or you decide from one second to the next to buy purple hydrangeas instead of white orchids as planned or offer a visitor a Campari and not red wine. These are spontaneous ideas, flashes of intuition from your inner Self, which prove your openness, and with which you are always successful.

The more you free yourself from faith in matter, the more your 7th sense can develop. You open yourselves to the supernatural, the intuitive, and the magical. You have confidence in yourself and allow your energies to flow unchecked to create fantastic situations not yet experienced. Your life becomes more intense as you approach your innermost fire, your primal love, and oneness. You are creating a wonderful life full of joy and happiness!

Realization through physical and psychological problems

Diseases are an expression of your mental imbalance when the flow between your inner being and the actions of daily life is congested. They manifest when you are weak and exhausted, forcing you to withdraw from stress and commitment and come to rest. Remember when and why you have been sick. And you will find that there has always been a good reason why you have had to withdraw. Pay attention to what your inner Self wants to make clear to you through a disease. If you have a cold and a blocked nose, your inner voice will tell you that you have had enough of something. Don't wait for the outside to change – only you yourself can rewrite your life as the author, plan it as the director, and play the role as the main character to stay healthy, to be in harmony with yourself.

Here are some diseases and problems that indicate inner disharmony.

Inflammations
Inflammation is an infection. 'Infectus' in Latin means unfinished.

The inflammation indicates a fire, war, destruction, but at the same time also transformation. An inner fire ignites to set something new in motion. So all inflammations have to do with conflicts within yourself and want to draw your attention to the fact that certain behaviors or habits are no longer valid – that your inner being fights against old things. Your body poisons and inflames itself when you hold on to the old instead of letting go and daring a new beginning.

Viruses cause many infections. A virus, or as in Latin, also poison, stench, nests itself in you and paralyzes your system. Hear the warning and recognize what you should change. Look where an infection has accumulated in your body. Take this place to realize which area you want to change. A good example is cystitis:

it hurts to let go. Or pneumonia: You get no more air for movement if you remain.

Stimulus

You know the feeling of itching before sneezing. It tickles, it itches you – something wants to realize itself. What relief, expansion, if you can sneeze then. The inner stimulus is the implosion, the agglomeration that pours out like an explosion. If a lot has accumulated in you, if you are 'irritated', if you feel anger and rage, then you explode. So realize that stimulus, itching, has to do with your positive aggression, your inner will, to experience something new.

Think: A new person is stimulating, he fascinates, or he attracts you. Something 'tears' you in a new direction.

Allergies

Being allergic to something means being hypersensitive. Feeling means perceiving. If you react allergically, you do not recognize your inner needs and desires and live in a constant struggle against yourself. You restrict your movement and do not allow your inner fire. You are allergic to something, to someone. Too much pressure ignites your aggression inside. If you do not let these energies flow out, they manifest through your body. With any allergy, you undermine your Self instead of trusting yourself and standing by you.

For example, you may be allergic to acid. You are internally sour, angry, swallow everything that's thrown at you. Then you become over-acidified.

In the course of my professional life, an allergy broke out in me, which manifested itself in red spots on my face, which I could only cover up with make-up. Every day I received well-ment advice from worried customers. Everything was of no use. The highlight of the allergy was in the morning after a collection presentation in Paris to which my boss and partner had let me travel alone. As a consequence, I abstained from eating and drinking many things, which did not bring any relief. Only when it became clear to me that I was inwardly angry with my partner and compensated for this externally with a desire for lemons did I solve the problem. Finally, I dared to say what I didn't like and didn't have to 'eat' the 'sourness' into me anymore. Years later, a supplier made me angry with his lie stories, and I reacted with a massive rash to lemons again, the background of which I recognized this time immediately. I parted company with this supplier at once.

You can also be allergic to 'dirt', dust, or animal hair. The pressure here is too much orderly love. On the outside, you pay attention to discipline and follow your duties, but your inner Self wants to let go and enjoy.

Especially in spring, many people are affected by pollen allergies, the so-called hay fever. In their inner being, like nature, they want to strive forward and get rid of the restrictions they have had enough of. This allergy will materialize year after year if you don't question your belief that the guilt is outside. You must change your attitude and your behavior- patterns.

Stomach problems
Troubles hit one's stomach. You 'eat' everything inside yourself, you have to defend yourself so often – you can't digest the too much any longer. It hits you and scares you, which clumps into a lump and manifests itself in cramps. Or something makes you so upset that you have to vomit. Question yourself whether you truly like or want what you are doing. Consider whether you are not angry with yourself because you are handing over your power to others. Stop this, reflect on your inner strength and instead stand by yourself. Free yourself from cramps and struggle against yourself through clear communication, for life is meant to be a pleasure.

Even though one of my friends had said to her former partner that she didn't want to organize parties with him nor act as a waitress anymore, she let herself persuade to participate once again. Three hours before the beginning of the event, stomach cramps and fever attacked her. This 'flattened' her in the most real sense of the word. The body gave her the answer for not having been strong enough to say no. Before going to bed, she recognized the cause of her nausea and was well again the next morning.

Overweight

Overweight – to overweigh something. You are one-sided, not in balance, and therefore sluggish and immobile. You wait instead of using your fire to burn the old and be open to the new.

If you are overweight, you have built up a 'fat' layer of protection during years of swallowing instead of living. Or you are addicted to food as compensation for being alone and sad because the outside gives you no love and affection, no positive echo. This too much in the pole of matter leads back to the fundamental problem: not to love oneself, not to accept oneself, not to trust oneself, and therefore to want to hold on and secure oneself.

Overweight also shows that you have a tremendous inner fullness within you. It is just waiting to flow outward. Finally, learn to love yourself, to praise yourself, and to break through your protective walls to be agile, mobile, and to live.

Constipation

Constipation is often associated with overweight. The intestine is a tube that is blocked. This tube has to be cleared of 'garbage' so that life can flow. You must digest what is coming to you, not (for years) hold on to it, but free yourself from it. Yesterday was valid, but yesterday is not today – today counts.

Realize, perceive, and let go, otherwise you 'slag', 'poison' yourself, and become weak, even depressed. Everything from which you cannot part catches up with you again, constricts you and prevents yourself from having room for something new. Like your apartment overcrowded with accumulated things, finally crushes you, so the adherence to old times does not leave you open to the beauty of the here and now. Let go!

Back problems

Many back problems are the result of tension. You are tense and overburdened. You have not only learned as parents to be there for others, and to take care of their worries and problems, you often even feel responsible for them. However, this does not help neither the 'YOU' nor the 'I' because both lack true self-responsibility. Recognize your misconduct, your wrong attitude, and stand from now on to yourself and your needs. No longer bend over for others, but strengthen your spine with sincerity and clear words.

Some back issues are jammed nerves (sciatica) that make you aware that you yourself are jammed and insecure. All the 'I must' overwhelm you so much that you almost paralyze, crippling yourself. You 'overwhelm' yourself because you want to prove yourself. You 'clamp' your spiritual development by 'clinging' to the matter and your faith patterns.

Indulge yourselves to the inner stream, the flow of life. Recognize what blocks you and inhibits your progress. To be tense also means to be dogged, to 'cramp', and to fight against yourself. Relax and trust yourselves and your inner baby.

A few years ago, I went for my daily walks with a group of dog owners. Then my back started to hurt. In the beginning, I tried to relax my muscles by bending down, which was of no use. The pain got worse and worse. So I went to a doctor who passed me on. After two years of different attempts with different therapists and therapies, I got the diagnosis that my back was severely crooked, and no surgeon could operate on it. I still tortured myself to go for walks with my friends until my old dog could no longer keep up. Finally, I was able to respond to my needs and those of my dog. I said goodbye to the routine. It became clear to me that I had provoked the pain out of the old belief that I had to be 'strong'. These friends were not friends. They didn't notice me and only talked about their problems. In particular, there was a 92 years old lady in our group. I had learned to respect elderly people; I picked her up daily, let her insult me, I even 'bent over' in front of her to tie her shoelaces, and by doing so, I 'overlooked' myself and my own pains.

My old dog died, the old lady died, yet I did not open up to new people since I was weak.

After seven years of suffering, in which I maneuvered myself more and more into the 'offside' because most of the time, I had to lie flat at home, the rescue came. A young neurosurgeon, who specialized in spine surgery, 'fell to me like an angel', I materialized him. He fixed my curved lower back with many screws, stretching it and giving the four intervertebral discs the necessary distance again. For me, the operation and the months after was a rebirth. I had to learn to move consciously! Today I am doing fine. The old acquaintances have almost all said goodbye, and many interesting, dear new people now accompany my further journey.

Joints

Joint problems can be associated with a lack of mobility in your thinking. Joints stiffen when you hold on to old views and are not open to new impulses. All diseases related to stiffness want to draw your attention to petrified behavior- and belief- patterns. When you 'drive' a car, you are free to drive in any direction. Also, in your life, you are the driver and decide yourself in which direction you want to go on. Now stop stiffening your attitudes, no longer depend on things, but become spiritually agile. When you hang on the outside, in the past, you don't live. You ride in the old fairway, instead of standing to your inner desire to move forward and thereby move freely again. Trust yourself to turn right or left to explore and experience new areas. Be honest with yourself! End unsatisfactory situations and move on fresh, free, and happy!

Bones, nails, and teeth

The bones give you hold. Through the teeth you have 'bite', can grab and attack. The nails stand for the courage to distance yourself and defend yourself. Just think of the cats showing their claws to protect themselves.

For years I bit my nails off. I always had to hide my hands and was very sad about it. But I didn't find the strength to resist and change anything. I left home when I was about 20 years old and the problem was resolved from one day to the next. I now know that I did not allow my aggression at that time. I was always eager to be a good child, not to burden myself with guilt. How happy I am today through this experience and the present knowledge that I can stand fully by myself and move freely without a guilty conscience.

Problems with soft or fragile bones and nails show your inner softness and 'brittleness'. You do not dare to break through old patterns and are therefore often forced to do so by a 'break', a decisive blow in reality. Not tapping into your life energy makes you lack strength and you become brittle and fragile.

Bones, nails, and teeth also stand for stability. To stand by yourself – understand. Just as a tree cannot become infinitely tall, the growth of bones also stops. The spiritual growth, however, knows no limits. As soon as you confront yourself with the mirrors in your reality, you find back to your true steadfastness and to your all-embracing 'I'. Realize that you are 'good' and 'strong', and you can dissolve your blockages and fears and get deeper into your inner worlds. Build up confidence in yourself and know that you realize the future out of yourself: everything makes sense and is right for you!

Heart problems

The heart is the center of your body and lies in the area of the color green, the planet Saturn, as you will see later. Saturn has to do with concentration, limitation, perseverance, and persistence, also with firmness and security. On your way into the matter and by believing in the validity of reality, your heart hardens. The outside offers you no 'security', and you experience disappointments again and again. You build up a protective wall so as not to be hurt any further. You begin to condemn the outside because you believe that it is the cause of your misfortune and suffering. You try to protect yourself all around because you are afraid that more and more will be taken away from you.

Pay attention to where you undermine your true Self and cling to outward appearances that bring you no real security but only fears of loss and disappointments. Your heart will warm up as you recognize your inner strength and security. Love yourself, and trust yourself.

For about seven years, I was in a relationship with an older married man. His marriage was, as I learned from different sides, a brother-sister relationship from the beginning, so I had no problem with that. It was a beautiful and happy time. Since his wife worked, we spent every day together except for the holidays. He was the happiest person I had ever known before. With him, I learned to enjoy and to celebrate. Because he didn't want to lose me, he often said that he would have to marry me to always have me at his side. But he did not dare to leave his family and with it wealth, security, and habits behind him. The relationship became too close for me and without a change in sight, I began to open myself to a new challenge that I materialized. In this separation phase, my friend began to cough, and the doctors found him with six narrowed coronary arteries, which had to be operated immediately. His heart became sick because he had said 'no' to a step into a new life and clang to the old collateral. A few years later, he died far too early of throat cancer.

Foot problems
Through your feet, you are connected to the earth – when you stand and when you walk. They reflect your inner stability and mental agility from which you fearlessly take new steps. You will only find your true independence when you understand, realize that you are building, realizing the outside yourself. That is why everything you materialize takes you further.

When you 'wiggle' realize that you are insecure, get bogged down, and lack stability in the here and now. That you have many ideas in your head and do not bring them to the ground of reality for lack of self-confidence. Learn to concentrate, to stand by yourself, and to use your energies specifically for your own advancement.

People who stand with both feet on the ground are rooted, grounded, and have the confidence to take a step forward. Do not stand still, but take the opportunities that your inner being reveals to you. That is movement and joy in life.

A younger friend of mine suddenly complained about pain in his foot. The doctor he went to had no explanation and strongly advised him to lose weight. I discussed the problem with him, and it turned out that he mourned his prosperous times and felt lost and 'poor'. He sent the little money he earned to his family. No longer being aware of his abilities as an IT specialist, he thought only another certificate would help him. After a few conversations, he realized that he had to stand by himself and be proud of his skills. Not only did he lose weight, he detached himself from his past and strengthened his self-confidence by understanding his problem. The foot problems blew away, and he managed to make a big step in his career.

At the same time, I had been wasting my time, busy revising this book, by pursuing other projects, which took away my energy for my most important goal. Through my friend, my mirror, I recognized my own problems.

Depressions
Out of fear of rejection, disapproval, and punishment, concerns of one's strength and vitality develop. If you suppress your life energies, they turn into anger, rage, and violence. You condemn aggression, and you, out from your faith patterns, do not live it out. With this, you deny yourself – depressions are the result. In Latin, 'depressus' means low, low-pitched/subdued, what you can relate to your movement in life. Nothing works anymore; nothing wants to get going. You are in the swamp, mud, dirt. Everything is grey.

From time to time, all people go through this phase of negativity, of retreating. It is the time before the transformation – the opposite pole to the real ecstatic being.

Do not resist the low vibrational phase, the depression, for the ensuing heyday will reward you. Remeber the movement in the '8' – it always develops from the negative into the positive pole. Therefore do not be impatient and sad when you are in the 'swampy' phase. Movement crystallizes from the standing, immovable. Affirm everything – because everything is right.

Many people are depressed when they are alone after the passing away of a beloved partner. They often overlook the fact that they have not lived independently, but have become dependent on the 'YOU'.

Your inner Self wants and needs this time of being alone and collecting itself, to be 'fit' for something new again. Accept the loneliness – be alone to become all-one!

Aids
Aids (acquired immune deficiency syndrome) is a loss of the immune system's ability to protect itself against infections. If you are not 'immune' to specific pathogens, they can make you sick. Immunity also means safety and 'immunitas' (Latin) freedom. So this disease can be associated with your desire for inner security and freedom.

Learn to find your balance, to connect outside and inside, and thereby become immune against attacks, secure of yourself. The outside is the projection of your inner worlds. Thus you can put aside the old belief in dangers from there. When you affirm yourself and accept the dark sides and the negative, then everything on this globe which you created yourself will be positive.

Aids is the cry for help – find security and strength in yourself!

The disease mainly transmits through the blood. The red blood is your life force and has to do with your creative potential. It realizes, symbolically, creates matter. Then its color changes to blue and flows back to the center. On this path, it collects the information from the body, translated, the 'outside' – realizes, grasps what needs to be changed to be healthy.

So take responsibility for yourself! Help yourself and let your true Self run free.

Cancer

Cancer is also a widespread disease that is still often incurable. In Latin cancer also means south, summer heat.

Cancer can be found in astrology as well. Its symbolism is the desire for change, for new beginnings, the urge for freedom. Cancers love the water, the sign of feelings and emotions. 'E-motion' is the outflow of what is hidden within you.

Listen to your inner voice and live according to your 'inner' desires and goals! Don't let 'poison dwarves', old beliefs overpower you and don't 'cancer' back, regress anymore, but realize your inner fullness! Live! Enjoy and affirm yourself and your life! This attitude warms your whole being, and you become the shining sun itself. Find your way back to your center – to the creator that you are. This is the meaning of life.

As already mentioned in the preface, my father was a doctor. During his long career, he had many cancer patients and always refused to answer when asked the question: How long do I have to live? From experience, he knew that 'miracles' could happen, that people suddenly became healthy. But three times he was forced by patients, owners of large companies, to answer their questions. All of them sold their companies. They decided to leave Switzerland behind and spend the rest of their lives in the Caribbean. After a year, they came for inspection and were healthy! For the friends in Switzerland at that time, they had 'flown away' and were virtually dead, but for themselves, they had changed their attitude, lived being alive and celebrated parties with new people.

These stories of people renouncing the old and the worn-out and daring a new beginning to enjoy inspired me. They showed me that real life and good health connect with movement and change.

Accidents

Accidents are not illnesses, but after an accident, you are also ill, reduced. Often you have to withdraw from the routine because you are disabled.

In an accident, there is often a prior fear of falling from a position, status, or routine. You 'materialize' an accident when you, out of inner fears, look for attention from the outside and thus can put yourself in the center. It is interesting to note that people in an insecure situation are often involved in an accident. Inner stress and doubts, negative attitudes towards themselves make them forget caution and mindfulness.

Become mindful, learn to center yourself inwardly, and consider which belief- and behaviour- patterns are hindering you. Recognize your fears and reconsider your strengths. Then you will no longer fall but walk upright in your world.

As described in the preface, I was provisionally classified for the last year before the Matura because my grades were not sufficient. While skiing, I broke my leg and found it wonderful that my environment took touchingly care of me. I had a lot of spare time and concentrated on the exams which I passed.

Today I am convinced that an accident is a relevant and useful experience for everyone it affects: you concentrate on yourself and the important things in life.

Anxieties

A baby is free. It may sleep, smile, give of itself, when, and how it wants. On the way to separation from yourself, you become more and more insecure inwardly because you believe in what you have been taught. Everywhere you hear about dangers and bad prognoses – the outside becomes more powerful than you, the doubts begin.

You let yourself be driven into a corner, you are in a tight spot, you have anxieties.

Many people know the feeling of narrowness in their throat and chest when they have to overcome to do something or to say something foreign to them. Others are afraid of flying, which indicates that they cannot take off to look at things from a different perspective. Still, others have claustrophobia, a morbid fear of staying indoors or on occasions where many people are too close. Fear of heights is about falling. It is the fear of not being enough and of falling back or down from a reached point. All fears are about the narrowness and limited liberty. Anxieties and phobias are disturbances in your balance. You are afraid of the outside and the negative. You lack confidence in yourself. So question your fears and build up inner security by thinking of the many positive situations when you have been lucky and happy. When you pronounce or write down these insights, your unfounded doubts vanish, and you strengthen the trust in yourself. Become aware of your power and uniqueness. Look back and remember the many times you have done great things and been free.

Ultimately, any disease can be reduced to a common denominator: Do not allow yourself to be 'poisoned', 'demonized', broken by your wrong beliefs that the 'YOU' and the matter is of importance. You make it! Find your way back to your Self by dealing with the outside, translating it, and learning to place yourself in the center. Become conscious through the reflection of your inner being, perceive your wrongly polarized beliefs, let them go and replace them with new positive programs to fearlessly go for the unknown. Life shall be an ecstatic celebration, full of joy, harmony, and happiness.

Do not forget that a disease mirrored to you by a 'YOU' also has to do with yourself. If you translate the external events onto yourself, you can recognize unconscious disturbances in advance and change something before you become ill.

Bach flowers

Here is the first described 'external' aid through which you can become aware of your belief- and behavior- patterns: the Bach Flowers, named after a doctor, Edward Bach, who lived in England from 1886 to 1936. He concluded that it was not the illnesses that should be cured but the underlying causes of sick people. Every disease that manifests itself through the body wants to draw your attention to specific inner 'wrong postures', inner conflicts. Dr. Bach was very close to nature and discovered that individual plants release energies that can uncover and balance such disharmonies. He made essences from plants he found to heal the inner causes of human misbehavior.

Bach flowers can also help animals. They take over the disharmonies of their owners as mirror images and often as closest friends. Through his animal, the owner can recognize and solve his subconscious problem e.g., by reading the texts of the drawn essences.

The Bach flower set (small bottles with concentrates) contains 38 flower essences divided into 7 main groups:
- Fear
- insecurity
- insufficient interest in the current situation
- solitariness
- hypersensitivity to what is coming your way
- Despondency and despair
- excessive concern for the welfare of others

There are various methods for selecting Bach flowers. Some therapists swing out the essences, others conclude from long lists of questions, and still, others let the person seeking help draw the essences from the whole selection.

Usually, four to five essences are selected from the 38 essences and mixed with diluted water and some alcohol. You take them four times a day.

A real change, however, cannot be achieved by taking Bach Flower remedies alone, but you have to deal with their texts. Because change happens through awareness – you must first recognize which ideas, thought, and belief patterns limit you before you can reprogram them.

In all consultations, whether with adults or children, I found that the detailed conversation with them made them aware of the repetitive situations on the outside. They could thus deal with their problems. By realizing the causes, they were able to make the necessary changes. I remember an eight-year-old girl who was plagued by great fears for a long time. The conversation made it clear to her that she had mastered many situations despite her concerns. She understood that she had to trust herself. The Bach Flowers she took every day gave her the inner strength to 'shoot down' a fear thought every time it came up and to turn it around with the new thought 'I trust myself'. Thus her anxieties were lost in a short time.

In a later chapter, you will learn more about the Bach Flower texts in connection with the astrological and Chinese animal signs.
    In whatever way – if you feel the urge to change, you will get the right tools for your transformation process.

Any sign that you materialize shakes you awake and shows your will to change your views and your life. **You alone are responsible – you are your lucky blacksmith!**

Crystals, colors, and diseases

In many books, crystals are associated with the healing of illnesses. In 'healings' for example, they are placed on the corresponding 'chakras' (energy points) to eliminate disharmonies between body and mind, outside and inside. If you use the crystals as a support for your mental growth, you can expand your state of consciousness by their respective descriptions, recognize the causes of your disharmonies and bring harmony into your psychic and physical being.

For 14 years, I was as good as married to 'my' company. But then I could no longer identify with my job and routine. Inside I was agitated, but I didn't dare to change anything on the outside. A big sports fair demanded that I, like countless times before, travel to Munich and take part in negotiations and discussions for days on end. I thought I was powerless and had to follow the rules as I had always done. But it turned out differently – 4 days before the trip I 'materialized' pneumonia, which freed me from all obligations. By this, however, a lot was going on. In the two weeks of my 'absence', I realized that I could live without the company, and the company survived without me. During the 12 days I had to stay at home, I intensively occupied myself with reading books about crystals, and my first exit led me to a fair where I chose and bought from a variety of crystals and semi-precious stones the ones that attracted me.

The illness that took my breath away and the study of the crystals opened my eyes and led me to submit my resignation to dedicate myself and my inner urge to spiritual growth.

In the following, you find the association of colors and crystals with diseases.

Black

Black stands for firmness, centering, stability, and innermost truth. It also stands for power, strength, courage, letting go, departure, and liberation. If you mourn, you are thrown back on yourself. You are forced by your inner being to reflect and prepare for something new. Often it is about becoming aware that from now on, you must take on the sole responsibility in your life.

Black reflects in the following crystals:
- Onyx, Magnetite, Obsidian, Black Tourmaline, Hematite.
- On the physical level they are used by crystal healers for:
- diarrhea
- dental problems
- bone problems
- foot problems
- feel in the hole

The black color symbolizes nothing and yet also everything. Out of the darkness, out of the night, the movement, the light, the exposed develops. From the condensation, the expansion. Pay attention when you spontaneously dress in black or dark. Towards the outside, you're shutting down, separate yourself, giving yourself the necessary protection, because your true Self wants you to stabilize, to center yourself to promote your self-confidence.

I would like to introduce you to a black 'stone', which I have only recently materialized: the Shungite. It comes mainly from Karelia, Russia, and consists of carbon, a fundamental element of life. Charcoal is known to collect and excrete toxins in the body. The unique thing about the Shungite is that it contains hollow ions, so-called fullerenes, through which it fills the body with missing elementary substances. Thus the Shungite has a great ability on the physical base to transport away negative things and bring in positive ones. For this reason, it is a miracle stone. On the spiritual path, it is symbolically the transformer. When you want to alter, you will carry it on you as a reflection of your transformation. This stone inspired many companions of my current journey – the feedback about the changes happening is sensational. Everyone feels much better, mentally, and physically!

White

The antithesis to black is white. In the crystals, white is translucent, transparent or shimmering, but also crystal clear:
Pearl, moonstone, topaz, rock crystal, zircon, diamond.
White symbolizes light, clarity, purity, enlightenment, expansion, real 'salvation being'. Black densifies, white dissolves the black, the negative. But do not forget that the dissolution of the negative is only possible by understanding and acknowledging the black. One contains the other.

White – the German word also means 'I know, I understand'. If you know, then you have found back to yourself, you feel strong. You don't look at the black side anymore, but positively and optimistically go forward towards new challenges, because everything is always right and good.

White crystals psychically 'help' to illuminate and provide assistance to accept your dark sides as white means cleansing, dissolving, clarifying, harmonizing, and strengthening.

On the physical base they are used for:
– kidney problems/kidney stones or gallstones
– stowages
– dizziness
– eye problems
– allergies

The diamond is the hardest of all crystals. Cut to a brilliant-cut diamond, it is considered extremely coveted – 'brilliant' – shiny, outstanding, radiant. Thus the diamond stands for uniqueness, enlightenment, cosmic connectedness.

The combination of black and white is evident in the bride and groom – she wears white, he black. The symbolism of the 'wedding' is the fusion of the two poles male and female, light and shadow, conscious and unconscious.

Through the confrontation with the opposite pole, e.g., your fellow human beings, you become aware of your shadow sides, can integrate them into your thought and behavior structures, and thus find your way back to true unity. Then you will be able to live the 'high time', the paradise on earth.

Blue

Blue is the color of Neptune, of water, of the sea – of the incomprehensible and infinite. Thus blue has to do with gaining clarity and getting aware of your inner worlds and depths. By freeing yourself from belief and behavior patterns and by letting go of the old, you become calmer and trust in yourself.

Blue Crystals are a.o.
Sapphire, Azurite, Sodalite, Lapis Lazuli
Blue has a 'softening', dissolving, transforming effect. Blue crystals thus are used on the physical base for diseases and problems like:
nerve pains
headaches, confusion of thoughts
depressions
high (blood) pressure
violent temper
Blue stands for healing, harmonizing, cooling, and soothing.

If you concentrate on this color, you seek harmony, peace, and silence on the outside while you inwardly experience the phase of the opposite pole, the color red, the fiery, and creative. When you are wearing blue, ask yourself if you are still blocking yourself or if you are giving free rein to your inner creative being.

Red
Red is the color of Venus and thus of the structure, self-love, affirmation, and all love. It symbolizes joy, lust, passion, openness, and also inner strength, and self-confidence. Red stands for activating, invigorating, vitalizing, and strengthening.

The red crystals are e.g.
Ruby, Garnet, Coral, Rhodochrosite, Rhodonite, Rose Quartz, and Kunzite
On the physical base, they are used for all problems and diseases related to the inner fire:
anemia
depressions
recovery processes
blood circulation problems
infections
viral diseases
fever

With red dresses, a red car you want to attract attention, present yourself and underline your personality. If you concentrate on red, you say yes to yourself, and are ready for extensions in your life.

Purple
The combination of red and blue results in violet, the color of Mercury. The two elements of fire and water, the poles above and below, inside and outside, black and white merge. Fusion brings transformation. If blue and red unite in your consciousness to purple, then you realize that your inner fire, the creative potential always flows outward, into the matter, where it solidifies to form and shape, to reality.

Purple symbolizes the primal wisdom, the depth, the innermost, and thus the whole consciousness. It leads you to higher understanding, to openness, self-responsibility, and subsequently to the change of your 'I'. Purple stands for breaking blocks and hence for dissolving them.

The Crystals

Fluorite, Amethyst, Sugilite, Sodalite
Physically they are used for all problems and diseases that have to do with blockades like:
fears
sleeplessness
migraine
neuralgias
stress
Purple brings mental balance, dissolves inner tensions, 'narrow-minded' views, and blockades.

The moment you realize that you yourself are realizing the outside, your fears, stress, and problems dissolve – you reach the true balance. Nothing gets on your nerves anymore, you are no longer 'irritated' from the outside, but it 'excites' you to be open to new experiences you create from within, which leads to real expansion.

Orange

Orange is the color of Mars and symbolizes activity, willpower, courage, adventure, awakening, and progress. This color stands for stimulating, vitalizing, and mood-regulating.

The Crystals
Fire Opal, Jasper, Carnelian, Topaz
are used on the physical base for:
abdominal complaints
indigestions
rheumatism
problems of the excretory organs
problems of the reproductive organs
kidney problems
problems of hematopoiesis

Orange corresponds to the male principle, which actively strives forward, for expansion. The old must be completed and dissolved to tackle the new. Thus this color, the combination of red and yellow, symbolizes the inner fire (red), which unites with the fresh wind (yellow). If you concentrate on orange, then you want to break out of your inner being, break up old structures.

Turquoise

Turquoise, the color of Uranus, is the antithesis to orange and corresponds to the sudden and to upheavals. You eat and swallow – suddenly, the food is gone. Or it suddenly comes up again. If you swallow your desires and needs inside yourself, they accumulate inside you into a conglomeration until they come up and manifest themselves in 'thunderstorms', strokes of fate. Flashes of inspiration and your intuition, the sudden perception and recognition also have to do with the color turquoise.

If you open your 'throat', then your mental ideas multiply, and you become able to alter your view of reality and your life. The strokes of fate transform themselves into sudden miracles that you unexpectedly encounter from the outside.

The Crystals
Chrysocolla, Aquamarine, Turquoise, Opal
have a balancing effect, connecting inside and outside.
On the physical base they are used for:
skin allergies
neck and throat problems
stomach trouble
nervous toothache
tensions in shoulder and neck

When you wear turquoise, you give yourselves the necessary protection so that your valuable inner Self can unfold. Orange unites red and yellow, turquoise blue and green – all four elements, red, green, yellow, and blue, merge in these two colors. The combination of orange and turquoise results in brown, the 'mother' earth.

Brown
Brown mirrors in the wood of the tree, which is a beautiful symbol for your way in life: you want to reach high up, you splinter into branches, but you can only stand to yourself if you take root in the matter, the earth, and advance deep down to the ground (water/knowledge). Often you will be 'felled' by strokes of fate. Only after having burned your belief- and behavior- patterns you can alter and to finally dissolve yourself into everything and nothing.

Remember the bird Phoenix, which only rises when the fire of transformation has consumed and laid it in ashes. It frees itself from all entanglements, can thereby unfold its wings, and can subsequently lift itself into infinity.

Smoky Quartz (called Morion when very dark) is the best known brown crystal, and people mainly use it against depression and mourning. This crystal strengthens the nerves and is thus relieving stress. Spiritually seen, brown 'helps' you to open your eyes to the dark sides and to learn to 'translate' the material side. In this way, you support yourself with brown on your way to becoming conscious, to taking over responsibility for yourself, and to building up new positive programming.

Green
Green is the color of Saturn and stands for peace, relaxation, centering, understanding, development, and security. Also for: balancing, calming, and regenerating.

Green crystal are e.g.
Emerald, Malachite, Aventurine, Jade, Chrysoprase, Heliotrope
It says that the green crystals have an anti-inflammatory effect and are on the physical base used for:
heart problems due to overexertion
stomach and intestinal cramps
menstrual cramps
migraine
liver problems

colds / Influenza
inflammations
hardening (rheumatism, arthritis, gout)

The color green corresponds to the earth element, to the gathering, to grounding and concentrating on yourself. If you have a time of too much behind you, you spontaneously focus on the green, be it with clothes or plants. You want to come to rest, because inside you are spiritually creative, active and prepare yourself for something new. As you blow up the recognized barricades, your positive thoughts become more and more condensed and can take shape and form.

Yellow (Gold)
Yellow is the color of Jupiter, the so-called 'higher sun' in astrology. The yellow color, the brightness combined with the warmth of summer, corresponds to the liberation from prisons and self-imposed bondages. By concentrating on this color, you achieve real expansion, symbolized by the lucky planet Jupiter. Yellow/gold have to do with mental balance, harmony, perception and letting go, logical understanding, movement, and expansion.

The yellow crystals like
Rutile Quartz, Citrine, Tiger Eye, Pyrite, Amber
are on the physical base used for:
infections
poor digestion
lung problems
stomach pains
fever
chronic diseases

Yellow is balancing and spiritually opening and 'helps' you to release yourself from fears, limitations, from hanging in old times and negative memories – golden times open up.

Lime green

The combination of green and yellow is lime green, which shines towards you from nature in spring. This color is in the center of the rainbow and pours in both directions into violet or ultraviolet. Therefore lime Green connects the material and the spiritual pole and symbolizes the bridge to the innermost Self, salvation, transformation, and thus the understanding of the real meaning of life. By concentrating on yourself, recognizing the logical consequences of your thinking, speaking, acting, and perceiving your inner needs and desires, you become able to alter yourself and your reality. Through the expansion of your consciousness, you will grasp the creative potential within you and start to materialize something new. Then you have found your true center, your inner sun, and you will radiate your light and your love into the world.

The spiritual expansion allows you to connect all poles and merge them into one whole:
red becomes blue,
orange turquoise,
yellow green,
lime green purple
and when
purple becomes purple
then black becomes white,
darkness light, the unconsciousness the consciousness.

In the following chapter, the rainbow colors are connected with the planets and the 'chakras', the power centers of your body. You will also find an explanation of your life path and the meaning of existence.

The connection of planets and colors

«The rainbow is one of the beautiful consequences of the decomposition of white light (generally sunlight) into rays of different colors (or wavelength). The spectrum of white light – whose primary colors are the famous 'seven colors of the rainbow', namely red, orange, yellow, green, blue (turquoise), indigo (dark blue), violet – appears 'naturally'. It is the drops of water floating in the atmosphere that decompose the light like small prisms". (Stéphanie Maarek)

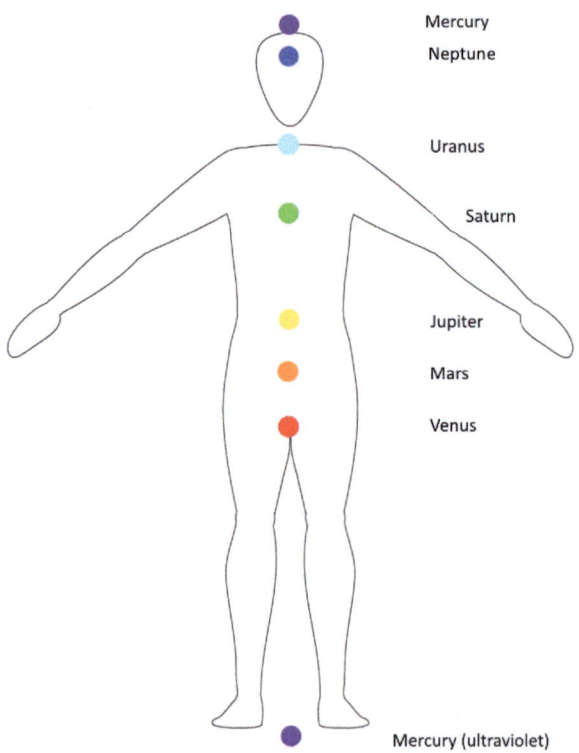

In this drawing, the colors of the rainbow are projected onto your body and marked with the planets.

The violet at the top of the head repeats itself at the feet as ultraviolet. This color is still invisible to humans. It connects through movement above and below, inside and outside.

The symbolism of the seven planets:

Mercury symbolizes earthly orientation and spiritual perception (ultraviolet below and violet above). It is about the intellectual understanding (you notice what is happening) and the opening up to new things, and thus about change. In Greek mythology, Mercury is Hermes, God of the air, and messenger of the gods. He approaches the environment unbiased, analyzes, orders what he has experienced, heard, and seen and makes decisions. Because of his eloquence, he is agile in exchange with other people. He is the mediating link, the bridge of consciousness between spirit and matter. He is also the seer who penetrates the veils of illusion and sees the truth. His mission is to bring light into darkness.

Neptune (blue), God of water, symbolizes the primordial instinct, the creative, the incomprehensible, the infinite, and thus also the chaos and the unconscious. In the negative sense, he stands for deception, illusion, and voluptuousness. In the positive sense for inspiration, spirituality and receptivity, devotion, and all-love. Neptune rises above the material, looking at things from a higher perspective and has the power to discard conventions.

Uranus (turquoise) symbolizes the sudden, spontaneous, the moment. Often people call him the unlucky planet because accidents, strokes of fate, or defeats are attributed to him. But such experiences are essential because they awaken the powers of the inner Self. Basically, Uranus is a planet of happiness because it promotes spiritual growth, love, and independence. Its mission is to stimulate life.

Saturn (green) is the planet of consolidation, security, and power. While searching for answers outside, Saturn symbolizes the division of inside and outside, of spirit and matter. But he also stands for concentration and gives each seeker the key to open the gates to the dark unconscious sides and bring them into the light – to find strength and security within oneself.

Jupiter (yellow, gold) is called the planet of happiness. He opens the way to thinking in 'larger' dimensions, to expansion on a spiritual level. He brings abundance and joy. Jupiter stands for generosity and the right progress, the achievement of goals, and logic. By becoming aware of the laws and connections in the matter, you find your way back to the paradisiacal, free, original spiritual state.

Mars (orange) symbolizes the masculine principle of pushing forward, of desire, energy, activity, and the courage to thrust outwards. It is the planet of procreation and of all that is 'printed' out, expressed in the matter. As the God of war, Mars stands for the will to attack, which urges the realization of inner goals. Your Mars energy supports the energetic action for yourself, self-confidence, and liveliness.

Venus (red) stands for the female principle, the receptivity, and the carrying out of new things. It symbolizes love, harmony, sensuality, and joie de vivre. Since Venus is responsible for unifying, connecting, and mediating, relationships fall within her sphere. She also reflects self-esteem, sociability, and the art of enjoyment.

With the will of **Mars** and the desire to merge of **Venus**, you will succeed in becoming one with yourself and all that is.

And at the feet again, **Mercury** – the becoming aware. Because the combining of above and below, inside and outside always stands for perception, recognition, and the subsequently following changes.

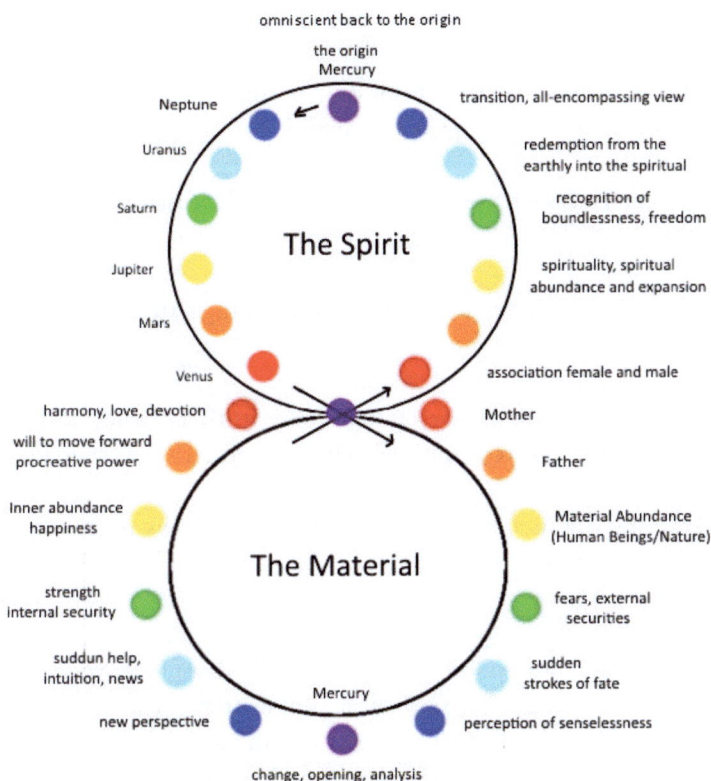

Your life path is described by the planets in the movement of the 8, as shown above:

First Phase
Your path before birth runs from 'above' to 'below', from the spiritual origin into the condensation, the matter.

Mercury: Your determination to become conscious of your infinite and incomprehensible 'being'.

Neptune: You want to free yourself from ignorance on the way through limitations and boundaries and grasp the 'chaos' where anything is possible.

Uranus: Your sudden idea to walk the way through polarity.

Saturn: You realize that this is only possible through condensation and a division of spirit and matter.

Jupiter: You open yourself to the way to the fulfillment of the set goal.

Mars: The male principle gives you courage and pushes you outward.

Venus: You affirm the 'becoming', your earthly existence, and are ready to carry out your spiritual Self to connect it with the matter.

Mercury (ultraviolet): You decide to follow a new path, which leads to your birth – you condense into a human being.

Second Phase
After having 'descended' into matter in the first phase, your path now leads you into the consciousness of matter, corporeality, and polarity. From the darkness, you rise into the light and, at the same time, into deception. You begin to build up the polarity of inside and outside, you and I. As the first projection of yourself, you create the mother – **Venus** (red). She gives you love and harmony. This part symbolizes the passive and receptive side of yourself. The second projection is the father – **Mars** (orange), your other part, the one of the activity, and the outward and forward pushing principle.

Jupiter stands for expansion, ascension, laws, and norms. You want more and thereby split your 'very own' Self and your knowledge into the whole universe. You lose yourself in the diversity you have built up yourself. You get scared and have to protect yourself. Jupiter is at the solar plexus above the navel. It is the place that you cover when you cross your arms if you are insecure. Thus you close up; you split your inside and outside, your unconsciousness and consciousness.

Saturn symbolizes your thinking and acting fixed on the matter. You try to secure and solidify everything you have achieved. Thereby you harden and 'petrify' – stress and diseases can follow.

Uranus: Strokes of fate destroy old things so that your life seems to be in ruins and bring sorrows, suffering, and difficulties. You are not aware that the new is unconsciously beginning to develop.

Neptune: Life seems chaotic to you. You allow yourself to be driven by fate, not having the will to alter. Everything is grey, and in the fog, you are depressed and not alive.

At the farthest point of your journey comes **Mercury** again. You question your life, analyze it, and realize that you have to reflect on yourself and change something. With this, your transformation takes place.

Third phase
After your insight (**Mercury**) follows **Neptune** again. Since the matter could not bring you security and trust, you want to become aware of the deeper meaning of your existence. You open up to the inner dark sides of yourself and are receptive to help.

Uranus stands for the sudden, the miracle, the awakening of yourself. You open your 'throat' to connect the outside and the inside, meet like-minded people, and find tools that will take you forward.

Saturn: You no longer want to cling to outer securities and structures and are ready to leave the old behind you. Saturn has the key to opening the gates to new knowledge, to the light. You learn to reflect on your strengths, to take responsibility for yourself, and to build up self-confidence and self-security.

Jupiter: By grasping the logical laws and the succession in the polarity, you perceive the hidden causes behind the reality – your beliefs, thoughts, and words through which you create your life. You become more and more aware of the meaning of existance and realize that by understanding and unifying the two poles, spirit and matter, you are finding your true balance back.

Mars symbolizes your stepping forward into the deeper depths of your Self. You can courageously shake off old beliefs, fears, and doubts and be open to new challenges that will make you aware of your inner fire. You now know that you are the creator of your reality, materializing that which leads you to the expansion of yourself. This makes you receptive.

Venus stands for this feminine devotion. You no longer have to fight, but affirm yourself, your life, and your self-created universe. Love and harmony reflect on everything that is. You only see the beautiful and the positive; also, the negative has a new meaning, becomes positive. You have found your way back to yourself and are aware of your wealth, which can now pour out from inside into the outside from where it echoes back to you again.

Mercury: You grasp ever-greater contexts and can unite the puzzle pieces into a whole picture. Now you understand that everything is one and connected to you.

Fourth Phase
Mercury: In this phase, you step back into the 'upper' circle, into your spiritual worlds and have access to your previously dark, unconscious side. You become androgynous, your female (**Venus**) unites with your male part (**Mars**). Your soul is in harmony – on and off, off and on are one. You create people, mirror-images that share your knowledge and are harmonious companions on your way back to your original spiritual Self.

Jupiter: You grasp the immense abundance, the spiritual wealth, the gold that you have within you that you can now consciously materialize all the time.

Saturn: You recognize boundlessness and total freedom. All fetters brake, and the matter begins to dissolve.

Uranus: You are free from one after the other and reach the all-embracing view (**Neptune**). You are on your way to your original state.

Mercury: You are omniscient back in origin; you are all one.

Tarot

The Tarot is one of many aids. The word 'tarot' comes from Egyptian, 'tar' means path, and 'ro' royal, the royal way. 'Taro', as you pronounce it, has the same letters as 'Rota' – rotation and movement. The word Tarot also contains the words 'red' and 'tar' – 'rouge et noir'. This reflects in the colors of French cards and the roulette. Behind 'game' stands addiction, lust, ecstasy, and thus being devilish. But in 'addiction', there is also the search. And that's what the Tarot is, a 'game' for the seekers.

Red is often associated with fire and the devil – with the negative and thus with everything you condemn based on your beliefs. At the very center of your being is this fire: joy, lust for life, ecstasy, and passion. It is your spiritual, creative power with which you can materialize everything you imagine when you detach yourselves from the limiting belief-patterns. Life becomes a game – you can playfully destroy and shape freely what you want according to your desire.

The black and the negative symbolize your shadow side and the unconscious. If you deal with what you want to condemn and accept it as part of yourself, then you no longer judge and divide yourself. By letting your dark and your light side, the conscious and the unconscious, become a wholeness, you proceed into the paradisiac state you have always been seeking in your life. Black is white then, above below, outside inside, and nothing is everything.

Through the spontaneously, unconsciously drawing of the tarot cards and by reading the texts, you can learn to become aware of your thoughts and belief-patterns to illuminate and accept the dark sides within you.

The Tarot game is composed of:
22 big arcanes
16 court cards
40 small arcanes, divided into 4 groups, wands, cups, swords, and pentacles.
The big arcanes also reflect your way of life, which will be explained later.

The 4 groups correspond to the 4 elements and the 4 seasons. The division into 4 groups you also find in the French card game. The diamond cards correspond to the cups of the Tarot, to the spring. The club cards correspond to the swords, to the summer. The heart cards to the pentacles, to the autumn and the spade cards to the wands, to the winter. In contrast to the Tarot, the French cards have 12 court or person cards (months), which, together with the 40 number cards, make 52 (52 weeks of a year). Each color has 13 cards (13 moon phases of a year).

In the following, you will find the relation of the Tarot to the 4 elements.

The 4 elements

In the tarot cards and the western astrological signs, you will find the 4 elements fire, water, air, and earth that you also find in the seasons, spring, summer, autumn and winter, and in the daily routine, morning, noon, evening and night.

The fire element corresponds to the winter, the night, childhood, and at the same time to death.

The water element corresponds to the spring, the morning, the youth.

The air element is the time of the summer, the noon, the adulthood.

The earth element stands for the autumn, the evening, the aging.

The relation of the 4 elements to the texts of the tarot cards:

The cards of Wands correspond to the fire – the power, dynamism, will, destruction and creativity, strength, and energy. The 'fire' is your innermost core, your inner sun. The sun has the power to burn, to destroy, and at the same time to build and to bring forward the new. Each of you has the sun within you. **Everyone is the center of his reality**, just as the sun in the sky symbolically mirrors the center of the solar system.

The cards of Cups reflect the water and have to do with 'emotions'. E-Motion is the flow that carries the inside out ('E' = ex and 'Motion' = movement). You let your inner being flow out into reality. There you see countless still or moving images. They are all aspects, mirror images of yourself through which you can recognize yourself.

The other movement is that of taking in, of understanding, of becoming conscious. If you are aware of this outward and inward movement (symbolized by the breathing and the blood circulation), your soul is no longer divided. You realize what you have realized yourself!

The cards of Swords stand for the air. Air, wind brings something new. When you are sailing and use the whinch, you want to make a turn, change direction, your view. You have to turn something around to become aware of the other side and finally come back to your starting point. The air element corresponds to the summer when you are outdoors. You are free – have freedom with yourself. To free yourself from boundaries is what the Sword Cards of the Tarot is all about. They are associated with the mind. Only with your own 'spiritual' sword, your understanding, can you cut up old beliefs and free yourself from shackles and limitations. While believing in the outside, you need the sword against the others, against the circumstances, and for your defense. And if you do not use the sword, you will be walled in by hedges like Sleeping Beauty. You sleep and let the movement and your life pass by.

The air element reminds you that you should be open to the new. Open to ideas and impulses from the outside and from within. Open to the exploration of yourself to realize your true needs and desires. Then you can free yourself from your self-built prison and understand the real meaning of life. Understanding – standing. Learn to stand by yourself, declare your stand-point, and build steadfastness.

The <u>cards of Pentacles</u> correspond to the <u>earth</u> and the autumn, the aging, the evening when the energies retreat. In electricity, 'grounding' is the diverting or returning of energy to the earth, the backing of the voltage to point zero. So to 'earth' means compressing, centering, and solidifying the ego.

The 'earth' is your world and also the ground, the dark, and the unexposed. Everything that is on the outside is in yourself! The cards of Pentacles, showing a circle or a 0, indicate alternation, change, and wealth. The more you grasp your unique 'I', the deeper your understanding of your inner wealth becomes. This 'grandeur' always reflects from the outside – now you perceive it. The realization of your inner magnificence and the change of your view brings you 'golden' expansion.

Learn to look at situations differently, from the other side, and to understand that both sides are alike.

Deal with signs, symbols, and fellow human beings and look at your life from a different angle. Become aware of your inner Self and realize that you are the creator of your 'earth'. What you think and let flow into matter through your words realizes! Remember: **The word through which the world is 'worded'!**

Here one of my most valuable learning processes: Every day, I'm out with my dogs and am probably not the only one who likes to walk in the rain. To 'magnetically attract' a pleasant walk, I initially tried to 'sweep away' the clouds and failed. I remembered that clouds and rain logically manifest when I think of them. So I made a new statement: It stays dry until… – and it worked. For years I (almost) always have managed to get into the car or home dry. Recently I wanted to celebrate my birthday with friends on a boat. I was only offered two dates for a trip to the Lake of Zurich. After a short consideration, I decided to go for May 7th and said with emphasis: 'It will be a fantastic warm day'. The big day was approaching, the weather was cold, rainy, and we even had to put on the heating. But on the morning of my party, everything turned for the best – sunshine and the most pleasant May warmth until late into the night! Once again, I became aware of how high the power of words is – they make matter.

Astrological Circle

You find the 4 elements in the zodiac signs:
- The <u>fire element</u> assigns to Sagittarius, Aries, and Leo,
- the <u>water element</u> to Pisces, Cancer, and Scorpio,
- the <u>air element</u> to Aquarius, Gemini, and Libra,
- the <u>earth element</u> to Capricorn, Taurus, and Virgo.

You will easier understand the 12 signs of the zodiac and their symbolism when you combine them with the cycle of the year and the months.

If you look at the appearance of the constellations in the sky from the south, the signs "rise" in the east. Your astrological sun sign corresponds to the constellation that 'migrates' into the light during the phase of your birth and is therefore no longer visible at night. The ascendant is equally calculated whereby the time, the minute of your leap into the matter, is essential.

The 4 cardinal points stand for the respective beginning of a new 3-month phase. North, which is always at the top of every map, is the starting point of the circle, where autumn becomes winter, respectively night begins. The east is the time of your awakening as you change from winter to spring. South, the beginning of summer, corresponds to the middle of the day, your stage on which you 'dance' outside. And you can equate the west, the beginning of autumn, with the evening when you concentrate on your home, your inner side.

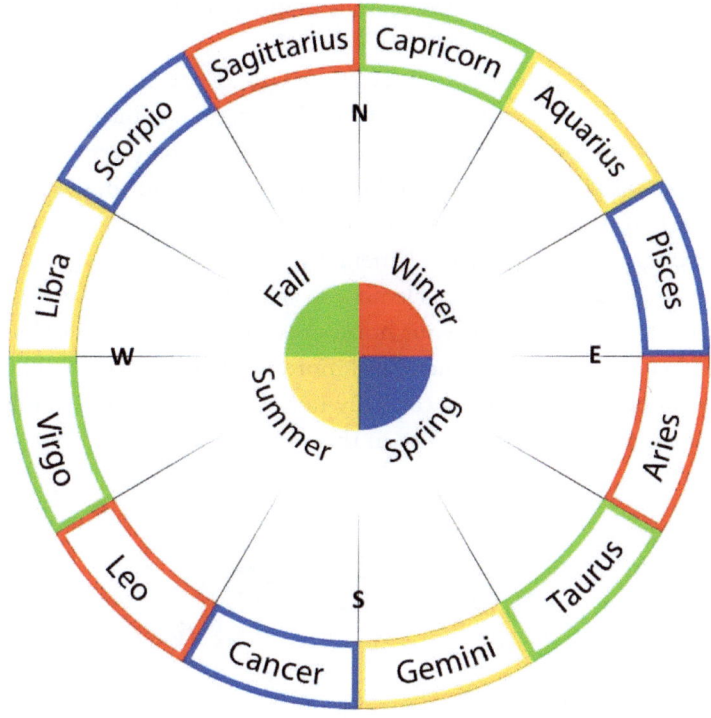

In the astrological circle, the fourth element is lacking in every season. In winter, you can see in the outer circle the earth element (Capricorn), the air element (Aquarius), and the water element (Fish), but the fire element is missing. In spring, the water element is missing; in summer, the air element and in autumn, the earth element.

If the missing elements are pictured in the center, an inner circle results symbolizing your home, your inside, at the corresponding season.

During the **winter** you have the warmth in the house, the red of the Fire Element. The cold air corresponding to the central Aquarius air sign in the outer circle reigns outside.

In **summer,** the warmth, the heat in the outside, is symbolized by the fire sign of the Lion. In your home, you often ventilate and bring with fans or air conditioners the air element, 'freshness' inside.

Spring and autumn are the seasons of movement and of balancing the two poles summer and winter.

In **spring**, the outer circle lacks the water element, the knowledge – you leave home, your inner being, go out into nature, move from the inside out as in youth, to gather new experiences and insights from what has been 'hatched out' during winter. It gets warmer, the meadows and trees become green – visible through the 'green' earth element Taurus.

In **autumn,** the earth element in the inner circle shows that you are retreating into your houses because it is getting colder, and you are centering more and more on your inner Self. The water element Scorpio is centrally in the outer circle and stands for the fog and the humidity in this season.

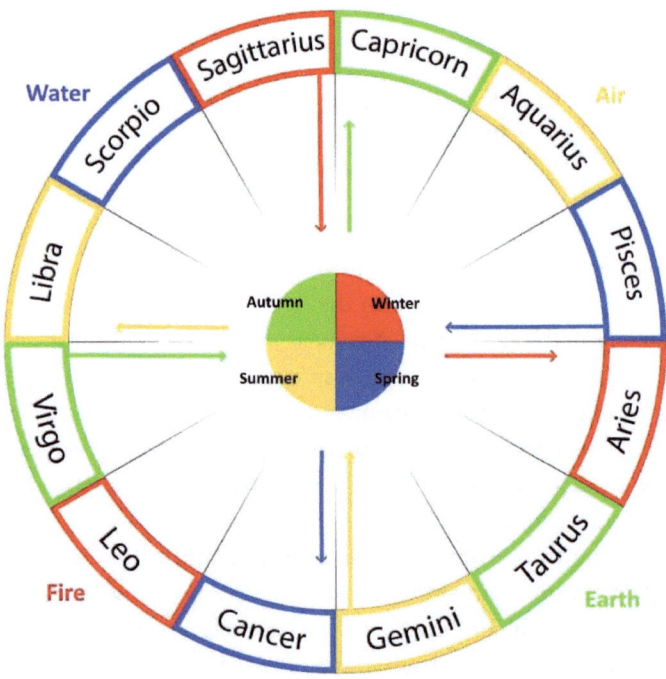

The above illustration shows you very clearly the movement from in and out, from one after the other in your earthly life. The last astrological sign of each season retreats to the center to be active there for three months and then to make itself visible again in the outside in a changed 'picture'. For example, the Sagittarius (fire Element, your will to move forward) withdraws its energy, like a tree, into the inside, to strengthen itself during winter and to create what begins to materialize in reality at the time of Aries (fire Element again). Only in the opposite pole, in summer, at the time of the fire sign Leo, do you experience the energy outside – the trees shine in their full splendor.

For a long time, you unconsciously create your reality. But when you become aware of this movement of in and out, realizing and realizing (like your breathing in and breathing out or your blood circulation), then the time has come to take responsibility for yourself and your life. You will look at the outside as a mirror of your inner being.

With your first breath, you step into polarity – out and in, in and out begins. You breathe in and breathe out. Here I want to remind you that the soul is the flow of this in and out, that makes life and death, day and night, black and white possible. The soul connects the two poles. The one cannot be without the other! You will then find your harmony when you bring the inner and outer into unison.

And so everything always has to do with yourself. For this reason, you are not 'only' a Leo when you are born in August, but you have the qualities of all the signs of the zodiac within you. Every morning you make a 'rebirth' and go through phases in life, in a year, yes in even 2 hours or one moment. The respective signs of the zodiac mirror this. Just as the sun does not illuminate the earth everywhere at the same time, so also you throw your light during one day, one moment, on different aspects, through which you can illuminate your unconscious side and expand your consciousness. Thus the more you concentrate on the momentary, the faster the cycle goes, the less important the time becomes. You can evolve in one day, yes, overnight, as fast as in one or more years before. One after the other – time will no longer exist – everything becomes simultaneously, in the here and now.

Back to the circle above, which symbolically describes your way over 1 year:

In <u>December</u>, at the time of the fire sign Sagittarius (red), you are active, want to complete many things before the turn of the yearn, and feel the desire for forward. You set yourself goals, on which you work inwardly during the winter months. Your activities take place more indoors because of the cold outside.

On the outside, in <u>January</u>, at the time of Capricorn (earth element, green), you perceive what you have 'solidified' inwardly in the autumn sector. This gives you the necessary security and inner strength to be open to new ideas and challenges in <u>February</u>, the time of Aquarius (air element, yellow).

In <u>March</u>, the time of Pisces (water element, blue), you have to deal with these new impressions and process them. It is the time of flow when your inner movement materializes mirror images in the outside. Situations manifest through which you become aware of your responsibility. When the time of the Pisces ends, the blue retreats to the center to build knowledge through the experiences you have during the springtime.

In <u>April</u>, the time of Aries (fire element, red), your inner fire and will, which you have inwardly strengthened during the winter months, come to light. You are entering a new phase and creating situations in which you courageously take steps forward and learn to stand to yourself and to your changed thinking and acting.

In <u>May</u>, the time of Taurus (earth element), your creative work 'condenses' into reality – flowers bloom, the trees turn green. Calmly and steadfastly, you follow your tasks, take responsibility for yourself. This gives you the confidence to tackle the next challenges that will lead you to the goals you had set yourself in December.

In June, the time of Gemini (air element), you are curious and open to new people and tasks that you create for your evolvement.

In July, the time of Cancer (water element), summer begins. The knowledge you have internalized in spring materializes in the outer circle. Now you no longer anxiously 'cancer' back, but resolutely and purposefully tackle something new.

In August, the time of the Leo (fire element), the heat symbolizes your activity and your will to become aware of your strengths through experiences. This brings you the necessary power and certainty to master everything with confidence that your inner Self is materializing.

September is the 9th month, the time of Virgo (earth element). The 9 always symbolizes a change. You evaluate the past in a structured way. You realize that you have to concentrate and thus gradually withdraw from your outside activities. It is the beginning of the condensation – the earth element moves to the inner circle where it is active until the time of Capricorn, at the end of the year.

In October, the time of Libra (air element), it's about balance. You evaluate between inside and outside, draw the balance. You recognize that the one and the other, summer and winter, the conscious and the unconscious, the 'YOU' and the 'I' have their validity. Through this, you find your inner balance.

November, the time of Scorpio (water element), is the time of the fog. The outside begins to be grey and gloomy, forcing you to illuminate your home – to come to inner clarity. The shorter days, the darkness, the unconscious sides, challenge you to focus your attention more on the core of things, events, and on the essence of yourself.

In December, the time of Sagittarius (fire element), you are active again. You are completing your tasks to reach the goal that you had set yourself the year before. With your fire, you are aiming for your next goal. Thus the old circle closes, while the new one already begins.

In December 1989, I moved into a new home, which led me to a man who moved in with me on January 1, 1990. It was a new beginning. During the autumn months, I had grounded myself sufficiently to take on this new challenge. The fresh wind and my openness brought me a lot of new experiences in February. I had to confront my fears, but I also had ideas, intuitions. In March, I took over responsibility for my friend, who couldn't or didn't want to solve his problems himself. In April, it became clear to me that I had to use my fire and my strength for myself and not change my 'mirror' but myself. In May, I was strong enough and was able to part with this man. He had 'pretended' to me my dark sides, my weakness, and my inability to take on responsibility until I was aware of them and no longer needed him as a mirror. In June, the time was ready for a new task that would lead me to my unconscious goals. I was asked to teach a course on the Bach Flowers, which was too narrow-drawn to me. The organizer gave me 4 days to decide if and about what I would like to talk on 5 evenings for 2 hours each. Out of nowhere, I had the idea to speak about 'We live to become conscious', which he liked. This decision presented me with a significant challenge. During the summer months, I worked intensively with my tools, the tarot cards, the Bach flowers, the crystals, which I wanted to bring closer to the course participants in the different evenings. The autumn months were then the time of compression. I had to weigh up the various aspects, concentrate on the essentials, and bring the knowledge I had gained through the aids to a common denominator. The course was supposed to take place in November. But it had to be postponed to January due to the lack of a suitable venue. Later I realized that I had not been ready in November. It was not until December that I became active to be able to organize my insights and to feel safe and well prepared.

Later it became clear to me that the whole year was focused on my growing spiritually, understanding more and more, and, at the same time learning to stand by myself. My course took place in January. Now I had to prove myself and put my insights into words in front of an audience. This was the conclusion of one and at the same time the beginning of something new – at the beginning of February 1991 it turned out. A course participant gave me the impulse to translate what I had said into a written book.

My will and commitment to having dealt with the aids and exposed my dark sides with them led me now into a journey into my inner being. I sat down at the computer, and 'it' began to write. All texts, drawings, and the then for me large incomprehensible contexts flowed through my fingers into the computer and came to expression on paper. It was incredible!

This wisdom was overwhelming for me at that time, and I could not share it with anyone. So the manuscript ended up in a drawer for a long time. In my thoughts, however, the texts regularly accompanied me, and I began to change my views. Today I know through recognition and experience that everything that came to me at that time is valid: Everyone is the maker of his reality!

Earth

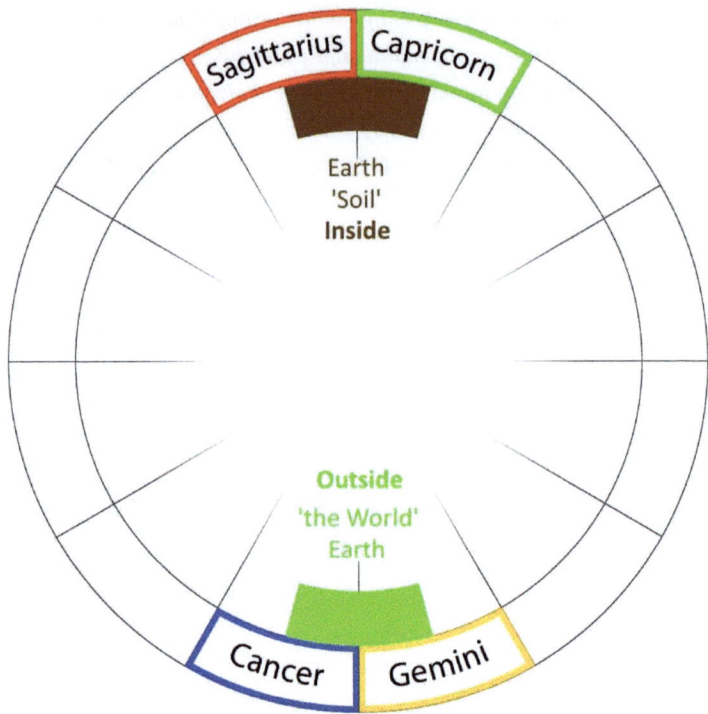

In this illustration, the colors red (Sagittarius) and green (Capricorn) meet 'above', and the colors yellow (Gemini) and blue (Cancer) meet 'below'. Red and green together make brown, yellow and blue make green, the colors of the earth.

On the one hand, the earth is the brown earth, the soil in which you plant something. It reflects your inner, unconscious side. This 'earth' rules at the darkest time of the year, the shortest day of the year. With the change of the year, it symbolizes the pole of death and the new beginning – the spirit as the counterpole to matter. The dead are buried in the dark earth: the grave, the bed of silence. In bed, at night, detached from the outside, you spiritually create the new, the morning.

But 'earth' is also the globe, the world. This pole is the reflection of the unconscious of you. It is green, the fusion of blue and yellow, and symbolizes life as the opposite pole to the brown earth. The green earth reigns at the time of the longest day, the beginning of summer, and stands at the transition from youth to adulthood. The youngster grows and starts to believe in the validity of reality. This is the time when the seriousness of life begins. You have scattered all your knowledge and your 'I' into all the individual particles of your world view. Thus you have built up limitations and restrictions. The outside, the world has become powerful and threatens to 'overwhelm' you what brings fears and doubts because you believe to be a nothing and not 'important'. At some point, however, there comes the point where you recognize from your innermost being that a transformation of thinking, of your view, is necessary. You open yourself to tools and people through which you question the earthly and understand more and more that the green earth, the world is full of symbols through which you become aware of the brown earth, the unconscious and the dark. This is the way: to connect the two poles, up and down – to return to the original spiritual multidimensional 'I' that you are.

Bach flower texts in connection with the western zodiac signs and the Chinese animal signs

The texts of the Bach Flowers draw your attention to many fundamental problems of your thoughts, belief-, and behavior- patterns. They, like all aids, awaken you from the darkness of unconsciousness and bring you clarity about what you can alter yourself.

In the following, you will find the connection of the western zodiac signs and the Chinese animal signs in the numerical sequence with the Bach flowers. The Chinese New Year is calculated according to the traditional Chinese Lunisolar calendar and falls on a new moon between January 21 and February 21. Therefore the animal signs do not correspond entirely to the western zodiac signs and the months, just like also the zodiac signs do not coincide precisely with the months. But the connections are significant.

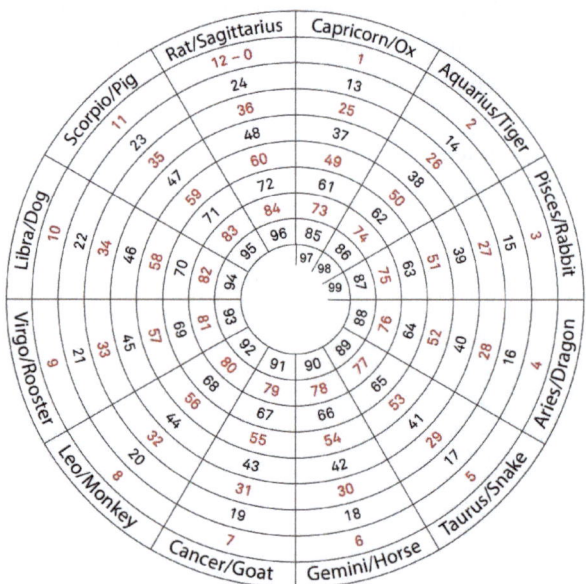

The <u>Capricorn and the Ox</u>, the first zodiac resp. animal sign, mean stability, strength, straightforwardness, and also stubbornness. They stand for the will to achieve goals and the willingness to remove obstacles. In a negative sense, they hold on to the old, to structures and patterns of behavior and cannot connect their inner needs with the outside.

The Bach flowers 1 (Agrimony) and 25 (Red Chestnut) indicate too much activity outside. This is an attempt to secure oneself and thereby free oneself from inner fears and anxieties. If you draw one of these Bach flower essences, then the challenge is to take responsibility for yourself and establish the connection between your inner and outer. Only by centering on yourself security and strength can be built up.

The Bach flowers 13 (Gorse) and 37 (Wild Rose) draw your attention to the fact that you give yourself up inwardly, feel 'empty', and have no strength to change anything.

All 4 Bach flowers have to do with making you aware of your energy, the source of all being, and letting it flow for you.

The <u>Aquarius and the Tiger</u> symbolize initiative and advancement, openness, ambition, the urge to explore and develop. They are on the move. In a negative sense, they are little concentrated, withdrawn, 'closed', and lack inner security.

The Bach flowers 2 (Aspen) and 26 (Rock Rose) deal with fears and instability. They are about building trust in yourself and becoming aware of your inner strength and steadfastness so that you can confidently tackle new challenges.

The Bach flowers 14 (Heather) and 38 (Willow) show that you try to pass on your unsolved problems to others and often withdraw out of bitterness and resentment. They help to open you inward to become aware of your fire, through which you will burn old things and step into the future with fresh courage.

The <u>Pisces and the Rabbit</u> symbolize the search for harmony, love, and affection. In a positive sense, it is about self-love and self-responsibility. Negative: You freeze in norms and structures, adapt anxiously, and want to 'buy' love. With this attitude, you sacrifice yourself and lose your valuable energy, both physically and financially.

The Bach flowers 3 (Beech), 15 (Holly), and 27 (Rock Water) draw attention to the fact that you misuse your energy, submit to inner and outer constraints, and suppress your real needs. You are frozen, hard, and intolerant to yourself and your environment. The essences challenge you to burn the severity, to be honest with yourself, to love yourself, to acknowledge yourself, and to take responsibility for yourself.

The <u>Aries and the Dragon</u> – activity, will, vigor, passion, and enthusiasm. Negatively you disperse and overspend yourself, cannot distance yourself, and cannot make clear decisions.

The Bach flowers 4 (Centaury), 16 (Honeysuckle), and 28 (Scleranthus) show that you cannot use your energies in a targeted way, cannot say no, and that you always sway between extremes, which makes you sluggish. Instead of moving, you prefer to focus on the past, being afraid to lose the ground under your feet.

All 3 flowers are about restoring your self-will and stability to make you use your energies for your advancement and self-realization. And to engage yourself more with the here and now. Doing this means the progressive enlightenment – the end of being enclosed.

The <u>Taurus and the Snake</u> show tenacity, perseverance, order, and discipline, but also mobility, the joy of life, and security. In the negative sense, the 'I' is limited, and the real needs and desires, the inner wealth, are dammed up. Thus liveliness and movement are lost. Becoming headstrong and stubborn are the results.

The Bach flowers 5 (Cerato), 17 (Hornbeam), and 29 (Star of Bethlehem) indicate that you do not stand by yourselves. You seek help from the outside, give up responsibility, swallow everything, and thereby slag inwardly. This makes you tired. You often even feel exhausted, in the 'swamp'. These essences support you to wake up, to stand up, and to strengthen the backbone that gives you support.

The <u>Gemini and the Horse</u> are mentally and physically agile, flexible, and adventurous. They pursue new goals, are curious and open because they want to understand and experience more. Negatively they show striving for validity, impatience, nervousness, and being tangled up in traditions.

The Bach flowers 6 (Cherry Plum), 18 (Impatiens), and 30 (Sweet Chestnut) draw your attention to inner tension, impatience, and distraction. These flowers are about spiritual growth, recognition, and letting go. For this, you must become externally calm to open yourselves to the inner movement. You want to break out of the old circle, out of the routine – it can only happen by a change inwardly.

The <u>Cancer and the Goat</u> symbolize the staying power, endurance, persistence, but also the urge for change and development. You are sensitive and pursue your goals from within. Negative: you do not advance because you do not stand by yourself for a lack of self-confidence and self-trust.

The Bach flowers 7 (Chestnut Bud), 19 (Larch), and 31 (Vervain) show that you are scattered, that you are wrapped up from the outside, and that you do not bundle your energies. Now is the time to remember your many former positive experiences. To become aware of your strengths and to stand to yourself. In this way, you will recognize your inward goals, pursue them with concentration, and reach them. By this, your self-confidence will increase and help you on your way to your self-realization.

The <u>Leo and the Monkey</u> show self-confidence, pride, personality, strength, self-love, and the urge for freedom. Negative: you search too much for prestige, you stage yourself egoistically and want to feel superior, to demonstrate your strength externally.

The Bach flowers 8 (Chicory), 20 (Mimulus), and 32 (Vine) expose your insecure sides where you do not stand by yourself. You look for affection and recognition, want success and power, but you don't really believe in yourself. All 3 flowers support you in recalling your innner power, strength, and abilities and thereby building inward security, self-confidence, and bravery.

The <u>Virgo and the Rooster</u> stand for the zeal, courage, observation and judgment, self-confidence, and pride, but also for the ability to go into detail to gain clarity. The negative side is: the search for external security, fear of conflict, holding on to the old, and thus being imprisoned.

The Bach flowers 9 (Clematis), 21 (Mustard) and 33 (Walnut): As long as you are dreamy and hold on to the old, you do not deal with the here and now. You do not trust yourself with anything; you are trapped in the treadmill of your life – in misery and soul pain. You must learn to look at situations from a higher perspective and realize that you have to discard the heavy backpack of the past and alter something to move forward liberated and relieved.

The <u>Libra and the Dog</u> symbolize balance, centering, self-realization, and self-loyalty. Negative: you lose yourself in detail, are distant, one sided, unbalanced, and loyal only to the duties imposed upon you.

The Bach flowers 10 (Crab Apple), 22 (Oak), and 34 (Water Violet) challenge you to look at both sides anew, which means to become aware of your inner world from the mirror image of reality. Do not isolate yourself from yourself and others, do not be afraid anymore to show your weaknesses and find your true Self through the living exchange of inside and outside. You have to center yourself, find your inner balance, and thereby create peace with yourself and the world.

The <u>Scorpio and the Pig</u>: passion, the affirmation of yourself, inner fullness and depth, movement and thus life, love, and happiness. Negative: You fall from the highest heights into the deepest depths, from joy to unhappiness, you take on burdens, are tense and hard on yourself, which can lead to overload and illness. You do not let go of your inner pressure and are not open for your inner desire for life.

The Bach flowers 11 (Elm), 23 (Olive) and 35 (White Chestnut) show that you should not waste your energies on vain, but should think of yourself and find inner peace to open yourself up for your center, your 'depths' and dark sides. There you will find your original vitality, joie de vivre, and passion.

The <u>Sagittarius and the Rat</u>: They symbolize the belief in yourself, the will and your striving for higher things and expansion, and the aggressiveness. You want to go forward, afar, and to be free. Negative: the 'I'-negation, doubt, self-sacrifice, and the being caught in limitations.

The Bach flowers 12 (Gentian), 24 (Pine), and 36 (Wild Oat) draw attention to your inner doubts and uncertainties. They admonish you not to exclude yourself from the stream of your real life. Now it is time to concentrate on your progress, to love and affirm yourself.

The symbolic 'circle of the year' closes – a phase of development from which a new 'phase' of life emerges.

As already mentioned, you can grasp your dark sides through the outside that you create. In this way, the zodiac and animal signs of your friends and partners also give you knowledge about which aspects of your all-embracing 'I' you are not yet aware of. You have everything in you!

The story of my back pain fits perfectly. My last friend was a Scorpio. Soon after he came into my life, my back pain started. In retrospect, I realized that in this relationship, I withdrew myself and my needs and hardened internally, which logically led to muscle cramps. He vehemently denied my 'other' thinking, which I had had since the insights in 1991, which often made me sit in silence. After 7 years, in which the pain became stronger and stronger, we separated peacefully. For me, it was a stroke of liberation. A visionary opened my eyes to the fact that I had to finally stop responding to the wishes of others and relieve them of their burdens, but should decide for a life full of joy. She encouraged me to take the manuscript out of the drawer, complete it, and pass on the wisdom because the time was ripe. This step into the spiritually and materially united view of reality brought and brings me up today great joy day after day. I can exchange my positive experiences with the many new acquaintances. And through the inner self-confidence and the certainty that all problems will be solved, I have also materialized the 'right' surgeon who was ready and able to 'straighten' my back again and thus strengthen my spine.

The way of life in the Tarot

As mentioned above, the Tarot game consists of the 22 high and 56 small arcanas. 'Arkanum' comes from Latin and means mystery or secret means. For centuries, the arcana has been available to interested people as an aid in the search for the truth.

The small arcana cards have already been treated in connection with the four elements.
The high arcanas, like other symbolic images and texts, make you aware of your path in life when you look at them in the 8.

Everything leads through movement, through experience and perceiving in reality, to the same goal. This is 'true' for the whole life as well as for a single day, because every day is life, just as every night is, translated, death and the creation period. And this also applies to every single moment, because the spiritual change is not bound to time and place and can manifest itself here and now.

Every movement begins at 0 – just like the high arcanas that start with the 'fool' (0).

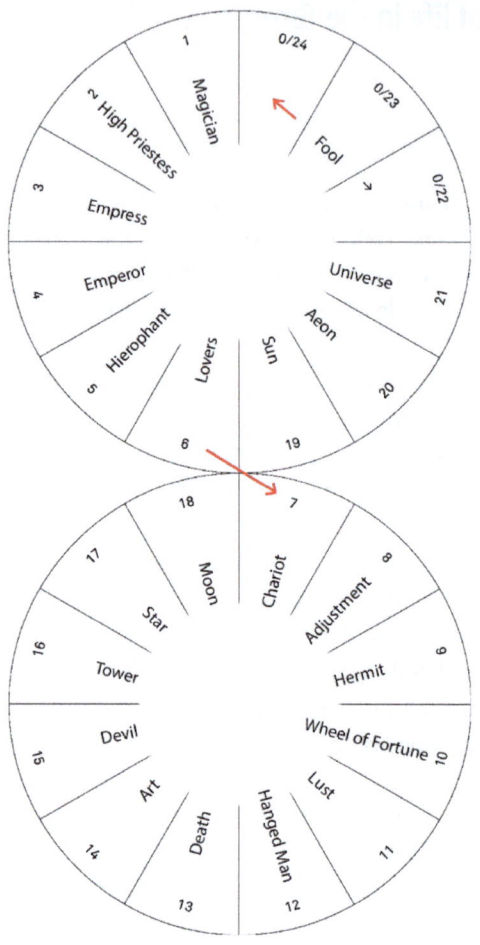

From the wholeness (0), you walk your way into the polar world. You develop through your parents (Empress and Emperor) until you leave the shelter of the house, your inner 'being', at the time of the 7, the 'Chariot'. Your journey leads you into separation from yourself. You distance yourself from your inner Self into the outer world, into the lower circle, the matter. At the lowest point, symbolized by the Death in the Tarot, you are so far from the 0-point, your center, that your inner baby urges you to rethink your old attitudes and beliefs and to make changes yourself. The way back goes through the Devil, the dark, unconscious within you, the Star and the Moon, until you find your Sun in the upper, the spiritual circle, and are conscious of your magnificence and your creativity. Then you know that you are the center of all Being!

The Fool (0) stands both for the whole, the all and the nothing. Also, for the starting point from which everything begins, and for the goal where beginning and end unite. Before your birth, you are everything, but you do not know. For this reason, you have chosen the path of polarity, which through **experience,** leads you to 'awareness' and brings you knowledge.

The Magician (I), like you at your birth, takes the step into separation from wholeness into a new level of consciousness.

The High Priestess (II) symbolizes the division into the feminine and masculine sides of yourself. Openness and receptivity, on the one hand, straightforwardness and determination on the other. As a baby, you create the first projections out of your inner Self, which materialize in your parents.

The Empress (III), stands for your mother, whom you make visible on the outside as the first projection of yourself. She symbolizes the feminine, your abundance, and creative power to materialize experiences that allow you to grow and expand.

The Emperor (IV) is to be equated with your father, the maker, and corresponds to the male principle – drive for action and going forward. At this time, you develop into a young person who can stand on his own legs. On your way into the expansion in this world, you split yourself again – you create the four grandparents who correspond to the four elements or seasons.

The Hierophant (V) symbolizes the teachers, advisers, and the 'wise men'. Through their information, what is right or wrong, you build the first belief patterns – you begin to give power to the outside, to consider it valid. Limitations and constrictions arise. You connect your experiences with the laws of matter and become conscious in this time of the movement and the succession – you have to take over responsibility for your actions.

The <u>Lovers</u> (VI) symbolize the belief that the 'You' is separated from the 'I', resulting in both struggle and attraction. You have splintered your knowledge and your whole 'I' into countless fellow human beings, animals, and things. For this reason, you are unconsciously confronted with the mirrors of yourself and begin to assert yourself in reality.

The <u>Chariot</u> (VII) symbolizes a change, a new stage of life. By entering the school, you take the step from inside to outside, into the 'lower' circle of matter. This outside fascinates you. And here you learn to master the tasks without the protection of your parents.

The <u>Adjustment</u> (VIII), often also called Justice, stands for the fact that you now move in the material circle, develop yourself in the outside, where you go forward, and want to represent yourself. You have created so much out of your inner being – you are becoming overwhelmed by it because you only give power to the outside and want to do justice to your fellow men. You are no longer aware of your magnificence and lose your inner balance and centeredness.

The <u>Hermit</u> (IX) goes his way to realize himself. In this phase you are immersed in matter where you want to find your 'I', your light. You diligently follow your work, fulfill your tasks, and concentrate on your own progress.

The <u>Wheel of Fortune</u> (X) or also called the Wheel of Destiny shows both, the imprisonment in routines and the possibility of breaking out from limitations into a new stage of life. You believe that you have found yourself, that you have consolidated yourself through your experiences, but you want more out of an inner desire. Since you have already moved so far away from your center, you doubt yourself, often feel lost, and hope for great happiness.

Lust (XI), also called the Power, symbolizes strength and the feeling of being able to conquer the world. You are 'grown-up', find ecstasy in the expansion on the material level, and use your energy for new climaxes like marriage and children. You undermine your true needs and desires as you adapt to the outside. Believing in its power, you thus give up your true responsibility. You will lose self-confidence and inner security as a result – you will have to fight, defend, and build up fears, which will cause you to be stressed and seek protection everywhere. You are divided within yourself and separated from your center – losing your energy and the joy in life.

The Hanged Man (XII) symbolizes the phase in which you are frozen in your views and attitudes and thus immobile and petrified. Often you are overwhelmed by worries, stress, and illness. Everything seems hopeless – a turning point is imminent. Your inner baby challenges you to leave the old behind and open yourself to a change.

Death (XIII), the opposite pole of the O – of life, indicates external changes and a new beginning. The phase of the 'Death' symbolizes letting go and freeing oneself from restricting fetters and structures to attain new freedom to unfold the true 'I'. In this time of death and rebirth, you open yourselves up for the step into your inner spiritual world and the YES, to yourself and the conscious life.

Art (XIV), also called Moderation, describes the ability to unite opposites. You begin to ask yourselves about the meaning of life, start to deal with polarity, with the negative and the positive, with the 'YOU' and the 'I'. The awareness that there are always two sides opens the doors to the dark, unconscious and shadow sides of yourself.

In the Devil's phase (XV), you realize that only by having believed in the power of the outside, you have been demonized, arrested in the matter, entangled in bondage and commitment, bringing you frustration, suffering, and fear. After 'Death' and 'Art' the time has come to expose and affirm your dark and negative sides. You become aware of your own devil, your inner fire and creative power, you return to your 'divinity'. Now you have the will to explore and become aware of the belief- and behavior- patterns that constrict you. With this, you open up the way for the new, for the true joy of life, the real pleasure, and ecstasy.

The Tower (XVI) stands for your change, your reorientation. It shows you that you must first destroy the 'towers' and structures that imprison you before the new materializes. You are now aware that you are the creator of your reality and check which old belief- and behavior- patterns you need to reprogram positively. Now you take responsibility for yourself and bring your new view into your reality by changing your actions. Get away from your habits and leave the old behind you! Tasks and trials in life that you create for yourself, you now openly pass to experience freedom, harmony, and happiness!

The Star (XVII) symbolizes inspirations, intuitions that 'flow' out from your inside. The star radiates as an independent 'being' from its center in all directions. In this time, your spiritual clarity pours out of your inner Self – your words let your visions and desires take shape and form.

The Moon (XVIII) shows you the ups and downs – the on and the off. By being aware of this movement of in and out, the illusion dissolves that inside and outside, the 'You' and 'I' are separate. It is the transition to your true 'I'. You can let the invisible and the visible, the unconscious and the conscious merge into a whole – your soul is in harmony.

The <u>Sun</u> (XIX) is the mirror of your all-embracing 'I'. You are aware of the meaning of your life path and now know that you are the center of your images thrown into reality – that you are the creator of all there is. With this knowledge, you have rediscovered the paradise on earth from which you were once 'thrown' out to become aware.

The <u>Aeon</u> (XX) symbolizes your way out of the compression of matter into the dissolution – into the spiritualized state. There is no more polarity – matter becomes 'superfluous'.

The <u>Universe</u> (XXI) finally brings the great liberation – you have reached your goal! Time and space dissolve, there is no succession, no limitations, no finiteness, no laws anymore – everything is right now, and everything is possible. You have traversed the path through the polarity – the mirrored 'image' of your true multidimensional 'I' and can create and dissolve it at any time.

And with the <u>Fool</u> (0) symbolizing wholeness and all, the circle is closed. You are back in your original state. Now you are everything! The 0 was the opposite pole to the 'I' in matter. The 'I' has now consciously become the whole.

Each path also contains the opposite way:

From nothingness (not knowing), the 0, the Fool, you build the universe with norms and laws, constrictions, and limitations (Universe). You learn to understand the outside, the ejected image (Aeon), and separate yourself from the all-embracing 'I' – from your center (Sun). You seek your happiness on the outside, where you are confronted with your shadow sides (Moon). You undermine your fantasies and inspirations because you believe that the outside is valid (Star). You build up patterns of faith and behavior (Tower), and thereby become more and more demonized by matter (Devil). You resist it as you do not understand that you project all your knowledge and essence onto the earthly

(Art). The material side, the outside, becomes so powerful that it leads you into fears, constrictions, and limitations. You threaten to die (Death) and are forced to a transformation (Hanged Man) by strokes of fate. Now you realize that you have to return to yourself, let go of old structures, and become aware of your strengths and real desires (Lust). With this, you take the step out of the treadmill of your life. You open yourself up to true happiness (Wheel of Fortune). You become aware that you find the light only in yourself. You are born alone – your path leads you back to your 'I', the All-One (Hermit). You learn to merge the outside and the inside into a wholeness. Thus you find your inner balance and penetrate to your center (Adjustment). Now you dare to put your insights into action and leave the old behind you (Chariot). You unite the masculine and feminine sides of yourself (Lovers), which brings you spiritual and earthly expansion. You connect the many parts mirrored in the matter to a whole and connect them with yourself (Hierophant). On the outside, you become independent, energetic, and creative because you trust yourself and are aware of your creative power, uniqueness, and talents (Emperor). On the other hand, you become receptive – the gates between inside and outside open. Your inspirations and ideas materialize. You are aware of your inner wealth and your creativity, and all your fullness flows outward (Empress). You rise above polarity and become aware of the spiritual state where the outside is inside (High Priestess). Now you are one with yourselves and everything that is – you know that you are everything (Magician). You dissolve yourself and the condensed matter in the 0, in everything (Fool). You are back in the primal spiritual state.

Forwards and backward, good and bad, inside and outside – everything is always the same. **Everything is always right**.

Numbers and the way of life

Also, in the numbers, you can recognize your life path.

The **0** symbolizes wholeness, centering, nothing and all. It can be the smallest dot and also the infinite whole that embraces everything. The **0** is the primordial state, the unconscious, and the whole from which everything manifests itself.

(0 is decisive in the material world – for one person $ 100.- is a lot, for another $ 1'000'000.- – the 0 is crucial.)

The **1** is the step out of the 0 into the new dimension. It is the line that divides into two parts as well as returns two parts to one unit. The **1** separates and completes.

The 1 romanized is **I** – the 'I', the identity, the individual. Every human being is unique, a unity. And yet also part of the whole. With the step into the matter, your 'I' and knowledge splinters into infinitely many individual parts. It is the beginning of the separation of the in- and outside. The path of realization that everything is **1** (one) brings you back to the whole, the **0**.

The **2** follows from the 1 because the 1 makes the separation and causes polarity, oppositeness.

2 romanized is **II** – two 'I's. On the way into the pole of matter, you split the conscious from the unconscious, the outer from the inner, the 'YOU' from the 'I'. Thus, there is a gap, an emptiness between the two units. You can also find this in languages: you understand one word only when there is a space between the words.

The **3** symbolizes the soul, the flow between spirit and matter, inside and outside. **3** stands for on and off, in and out – for your breath, the breath of life. It is also reflected in the course of your blood, your elixir of life. The soul makes life possible. As a flow, it brings movement – in the material world, the succession, the consequence, one follows the other.

When you add up the 24 hours of a day, 1 + 2 + 3+ ... + 24, then the result is 300.

That's worth a notice! It symbolizes the Trinity, the 'I', the outside and the inside, which only you yourselves can unite into the Trinity by becoming aware that everything is one.

The **4** (4 parts form a 0) reflects in the seasons, the elements and the wind directions. **4** parts result from a vertical and a horizontal line – the cross. In astrology, the cross symbolizes matter.

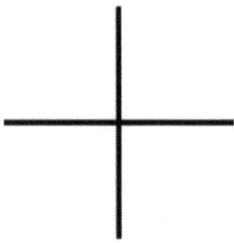

The 2 lines of the cross, horizontal and vertical, have a beginning and an end. If you place the vowels A, E, 0, and U at the beginning and endpoints, then the time, start (**a**wakening) and **e**nd, and space, above and below (**o**ver and **u**nder) result from it. The lines, 1 or the vowel **I**, separate above and below, yesterday and tomorrow. **I** (the 'I') are you yourselves – you set yourselves limits.

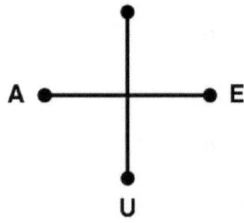

As long as you only believe in the earthly, you build barriers and walls that will restrict you. If you expand your consciousness, then you will be able to realize them and to break through your limitations. By concentrating on the central point of the cross, on yourself, you become aware that everything connects to you – you materialize everything yourself.

The **5** stands for the overview and vice versa for the subconsciousness. You have **5** fingers; the thumb summarizes the 4 others what enables you to grasp things. The **5** you can also find in the pyramid, where the central point above summarizes everything.

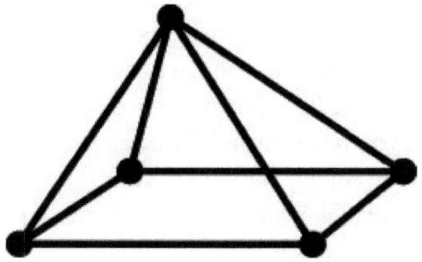

The pyramid symbolizes the 3 dimensions and thus, the advanced view. Form and shape, as well as the daily events, can be seen from 'above', from a higher view – you can get an overall image and take stock of your momentary life. Seen this way, the **5** is the superconsciousness that exposes your subconsciousness.

At **6** a.m. and evening, the two poles of the male and female principle connect. At this time of the day and night, the sun rises and sets. Thus the **6** stands for the balance between the outflow to the outside and the inflow into the center.

When you are divided within yourself and separate the 'You' and the 'I', you go out in search of your second half. You have a deep desire to merge the two poles, which you seek in sex (**6** – six). You are enamored, and through this, you love wrongly and give away your self-love. The disappointments and frustrations, instead of fulfillment and lust, can follow because you are deceiving yourself.

The **6** symbolizes movement and thus power and energy. Become aware through the **6**, in which situations, for which behavior patterns you waste your energy, instead of letting it flow for yourself and your advancement.

The **7** was considered 'perfect' in ancient times. You find the **7** in the days of the week, in the colors of the rainbow, on the tone scale, and in the wonders of the world. In the history of creation, the seventh day is the day of rest and of looking back on what has already been achieved. **7** stands for a conclusion, a dissolution, at the same time also for the preparation of something new.

On the way from **1** to **6**, you have become aware that you are the creator of your reality. Now it is time to use your new consciousness that you have reached through the deeds in your life. Your many achievements symbolize your inner wealth. You are incredibly rich when you are conscious of your creative potential.

Your advancement now is, like a child, free of belief- and behavior- patterns, spontaneously and naively – naive, native. You come closer to your true nature, your original state.

The **8** merges two circles, spirit and matter, as well as the 3 and its reflection. The **8** symbolizes the movement of creating and grasping. The consciousness of realization and realization brings the true balance, harmony. You now know that without passing through one side, you cannot grasp the other. And that only by dealing with the matter and its laws, you understand the opposite pole, the spirit, being everything and for which everything is possible.

Now you step up to the **9**, the mirrored 6. It symbolizes the change – the movement into a new dimension. On your path of life, this is the step into the dissolution of matter. You are now a holistic, all-embracing, and all-knowing 'I' because you have realized that everything is one.

The 'One and All', the 'All-One Being', is the **10**. When you draw a line around the whole earth from one point, this line meets again with the starting point; it becomes a circle, a big 0, where beginning and end connect. There is neither a beginning nor an end, neither up nor down, neither space nor time – everything is one and 'I.O.' (In order).

Source and back to the source

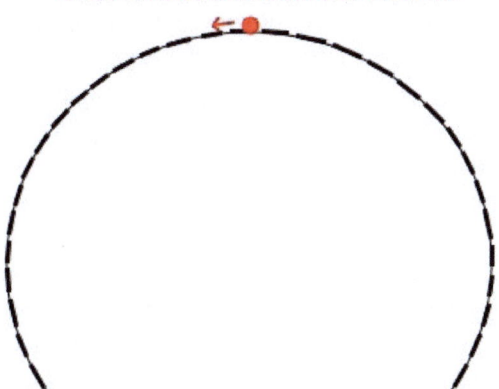

A = 0 (zero)

Everything makes sense – including the letters and numbers that are symbolic signs and want to show you something. You yourself realize everything that is to realize what you can change to live happily and freely. Words with which you call the images reflected on the outside, the names of your closest people, friends, and the numbers, which are also words when spoken out, accompany you daily. Every person, even your pet, has a name with which you address him/her. Everyone also has a passport-, an identity-number. Cars, your place of residence, your house, your date of birth, and your age are marked and expressed by numbers.

The following interpretations of the letters and numbers give you hints in your daily life why you materialize your inner world on the outside, in the 'YOU', why you live in this city, why you travel to this place, or why you have decided for a specific type of car. You have created these signs to capture yourselves.

First, you will find an explanation of why the letters and numbers are also represented in the 8.

As you can see, the 26 letters of the alphabet coincide with the cycle of one day. A is 0, B is 1, C is 2, and so on. In each period, beginning and end, or end and beginning, flow into each other. This is shown in the diagram, where the above Y/24 coincides with A/0 and Z/25 with B/1.

A and 0 contain everything. For example, the still unborn baby is already before birth, an independent, perfect, but not yet visible being. This perfection, wholeness, is symbolized by A, 0. With delivery, the baby materializes at the top of the 8 where B begins. Then it goes through its 1st year of life to its 1st birthday

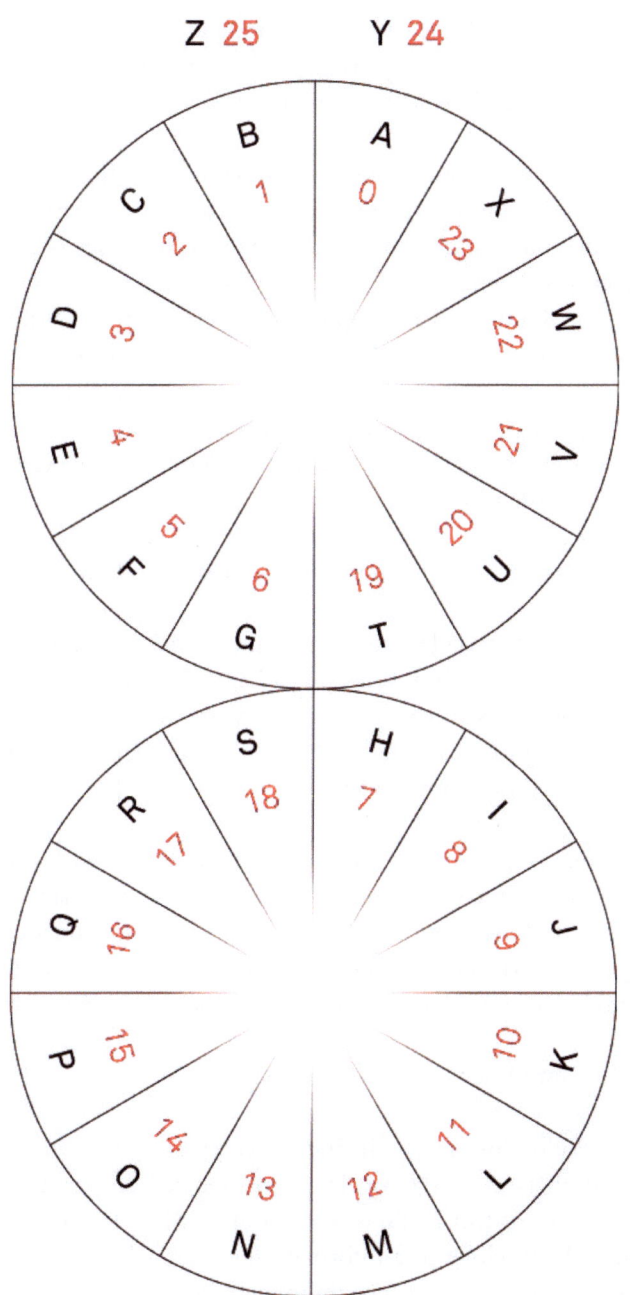

where C and its 2nd year of life begin, and so on. For the mother, her circle has not yet finished with the birth. Until the end of phase Z, her child is still utterly dependent on her.

If you look at the circle concerning your own life, then the Y (phase 24) means recognizing the stagnating life situation at the moment and then grasping what you want to change. Again the highest point of the circle is the moment when you are sure and e.g., give notice, and a new phase in your life begins. With your thoughts and partly also deeds, you are already in the new cycle in time B, but at the same time, you have to finish in the 25th, the Z-phase, the old, like with a period of notice. Only then will you be strengthened and free for new challenges, adventures, and the new cycle.

In this chapter, you'll come back to the question: WHY?

Have you ever wondered why a friend has this or that name? Or were you ever curious why you call a tree a tree and not otherwise? You yourself have created this word and the image of the tree. Everything that is has and makes sense – if you want to become conscious, you will find it.

Everyone is the center – the sun, around which everything revolves. You as the sun expose what you, as the author, have created spiritually. Now is the time to reveal the dark, unconscious sides of your 'I'! Always ask yourself: Why – the answers are within yourself and an echo of your original holistic Self and knowledge.

Nomen est Omen – the name is a sign.

In the following, you will find the interpretation of the letters and numbers. As you have already recognized, the 0, the origin, contains everything. Thus is also in the initial letter of words, especially of names, the information essential for you to expose your unconscious sides. For those who are not interested in why this or that happens, the 0 remains a little dot, nothing. Once you have realized, however, that it is valuable to become aware of your inner and unconscious dark sides, the 0 changes step by step to all-embracing knowledge and all-one being.

Everything happening in your reality now has been realized by yourself, thrown out into the matter, and is a gift of your inner Self. Your fellow players, the 'YOU's, are your helpers in becoming aware of your inside and your wholeness. You have 'orchestrated' them all for your growing, changing your attitudes and your actions, and your returning to your source.

Take, for example, the words king, emperor or lion – they all want to reflect your grandeur, are aspects of your self.

Now sit down comfortably. Open the following pages with the initials. Chose the initial of your counterparts who are closest to you, who you meet in the here and now. The letter with which you are addressing someone is correct. Find also answers when you meet someone or travel to a place that makes an impression or seems memorable (who or what is worthy of remembering). Just be open, let what you read work, **throw the light on yourself, become conscious, and act differently** – this is how you bring about movement and change!

I remember some 'aha' experiences in terms of names and initials. I moved from the country to the city where I hardly knew anyone. Among my first acquaintances was Maria. Shortly afterward, girlfriends whose names all began with an M surrounded me. Only when I was conducted around like a maid by a Magda did I notice that I behaved submissively. The text to M gave me the strength to incorporate 'I man, I can' into my thinking, to strengthen myself, and to give less power to the outside. At the same time, I met an Eliane. Her name made it clear to me that I had to free myself from old faith patterns ('ex Liane' – a plant that grows upon other plants or vertical structures because it cannot carry itself) and could trust my own power anew.

Sometime later a 'YOU' with the initial letter L came into my life. The stories from her life as a 'louse girl' and her laughter made me aware that now was the time to take life more 'easier' and finally laugh at myself again.

Many names, people, have accompanied my path. With each change, some of them moved away, and others filled the gaps. At the moment, it is F's that are close to me – fresh, free, cheerful…

The past was complicated enough – now let your path to spiritual growth be 'simple', easy, and have fun. Be amazed and smile at yourself as you uncover aspects and attitudes that you have not been aware of before on this new journey into your inner Self. Recognize what you are upset about – what should inspire you anew! Capture why you have not respected yourself enough, misused your energies, not really lived, and not really loved yourself! Become mindful – you are the creator, the doer of all that is, and therefore bear full responsibility! **Each of you is the center of all being and the most precious thing that exists!**

Have fun!

ABBREVIATED VERSION

A / 0   is the **awakening** of your **authentic** Self

B / 1   is to **become** free of imposed **boundaries** and to **be** ready to **burst** into new beginnings

C / 2   is to **concentrate** on the positive. To know: I **can!**

D / 3   is to **dare** to step out of the **dark** into light

E / 4   is to use your **energy** to **end** that which no longer serves you and to **encourage** the new

F / 5   is to **feel fresh, free**, and to be **full** of energy to enjoy **fun**

G / 6   is to see the **good** in everything there is and thus to **generate glorious** moments

H / 7   is to stop **hoping** but **heartfully heading** into **happiness**

I / 8   is to listen to the **inner** voice and to **irrevocably** stand to the **'I'** – **I am** important

J / 9   is to find back to **juvenility, joy** and **jubilation**

K / 10   is to grab the **keys** to open doors for more **knowledge**

L / 11   is to **live** with **lust** and **love**

M / 12   is to realize that you are **mentally** the **maker** of **matter**

N / 13   is to realize that each point of **nothing** or **nowhere** brings the **new**

O / 14   is to go **out**, to jump **over obstacles**, and to be **open** and **optimistic**

P / 15   is to recognize your **potential**, to affirm **your power**, and to be **positive**

Q / 16   is to **quit quarrels** and to open up to your **queries** why all happens

R / 17   is to **realize** and **realize**! To **respect** yourself and to **recognize** how **rich** you are

S / 18   is to build up the inner **security** and **strength** instead of continuing to cling to external **secureness**

T / 19   is to **trust** in yourself and in your **temper** to achieve **triumphs**

U / 20   is to **understand** and to **unfold** your Self

V / 21   is to recognize your **value**, to live your **vitality**, and to be open for **victory**

W / 22   is to affirm your **worth**, **your wealth**, and to know **what** you **want**

X / 23   is to concentrate and to bring everything to one central point

Y / 24   is to say **YES** to **yourself** and to bring clear insights and connections down to reality

Z / 25   is to end a circle, to close a **zero**, and to be ready to fulfill your next goals with new **zeal**

A / 0

ABIGAIL, ADAM, AILEEN, ALAN, ALISSON, ANDREW, ANGELA...
AFRICA, AMERICA, ARGENTINA, AUSTRALIA, ALABAMA, ARKANSAS, ARIZONA...
ACHILLES TENDON, ACCIDENT, ARMS, ANKLE, ANOREXIA, ARTHRITIS, AIDS...

A and 0 stands for the awakening of your authentic Self.

There might not be obvious hints yet, but your inner Self is ready for new experiences. Like a baby **already** complete in the belly of the mother, it is not yet visible. Situations with **A**'s and **0**'s **always** indicate that something new is developing and preparing to show itself. The **A**'s and the **0** stand for the positive **aggression** and the inner incentive for **advancement** and **achievement** of new goals. The old must dissolve as your inner baby chooses to **alter** and take a new path.

In the negative sense, you are going through the same experiences **again and again**. You are **afraid** of change and would rather **abide** by a monotonous life. You feel **abused** and **abandoned**. You **accuse** others and external factors of your fate. In many ways, you **act against** yourself and **abstain** from life. This often makes you negatively **aggressive** instead of using your positive **aggression** for transformation.

Be **aware** of **A**'s and **0**'s that show up in your reality as they are **always** a sign that you should become **active** yourself and trust that you can **alter** your old beliefs and behaviors right now. Nothing that happens is **aimless**.

It's time to **accept** yourself and **all** that is. You **are** the center and creator of your reality and only you yourself can **accomplish** the change.

In positive **A** and **0** situations, you have **altered** your **attitude** towards yourself and the outside. You **acknowledge all** there is as you know that you, as the **author**, create your self-perceived reality. You are **aware** of being the center. You, therefore, are **able** to change your life for the better **anytime** if you so desire. You don't feel **alone anymore**, but at one with **all**! The **atmosphere** surrounding you is **amiable** and full of **abundance**. Instead of hanging around with old agitating acquaintances, your golden **aura attracts** new **affectionate** friends. Together you **are able** to **appreciate** and **animate** yourself to **anticipate** the 'birth' of new experiences — you know that life is an **amazing adventure!**

B / 1

BARBARA, BEN, BERYL, BILLY, BOBBY, BRIDGET…
BAHAMAS, BELGIUM, BIRMINGHAM, BERLIN, BARCELONA…
BREAST, BLADDER, BACK, BRAIN, BONES, BOTTOM, BRONCHITIS…

B and 1 stands for your becoming free of self-imposed boundaries and you being ready to burst into new beginnings.

B and **1** symbolize harmony and inner **balance**. The **1** is numerically the real **beginning** after the 0 (zero), the nothing or the all. When the **baby** reaches its first **birthday**, it starts to walk on its own feet and move independently.

In a negative **B** and **1** phase, you **behave** according to the ideas of others and forget your own needs. Although you often get **bored**, you do not dare to say no or yes to yourself. Instead of moving forward you tend to step **backward**. As you continuously focus on your negative past, you feed your emotional and physical body with unhealthy energy. Because you unconsciously make yourself small and give your power away, you **believe** you have to apologize all the time and say please for everything. **Blind** and deaf to the positive things that happen on a daily **basis**, you do not see the necessity of changing your old rigid **beliefs**. It's time now to stand up for yourself and **break** through the old **behavior** patterns and **blocks** you originally **built** for yourself.

In the positive, **B** and **1** symbolize your inner **balance**. You know now that the outside is the mirror of your inside. As you **boldly** go through life, you can **banish** negativity at once. You can **blow** away old structures and any doubts. You trust your inner **baby** and your intuition as you know that this **brings** what is best for you. You also recognize your **basic** needs and **bravely** take action to fulfill them. Like a **bird,** you can look at situations from an elevated view and grasp the connections. You feel **blessed**. Now you can **blossom** and **bloom**. Every day you celebrate a new **birthday**. Your life is **brilliant** and full of **beneficence**!

C / 2

CARINA, CARL, CAROLINE, CHARLES, CHRIS, CINDY, CLARK...
CHILE, CUBA, CHINA, CALIFORNIA, COLORADO, CHICAGO...
CHEST, CHIN, CHOLESTEROL PROBLEMS, CANCER, CYSTITIS, COLD...

C and 2 stand for your concentration and for your knowing: I can!

In the **2**nd year of life, the **change** from baby to **child** occurs. As in **cell** division, it is in this time when human beings divide themselves into both feminine (Mother) and masculine (Father) parts. With this, the world of polarity begins. The child is not androgynous anymore – it is only half of the **complete circle**, the '0' (Zero).

In negative **C** and **2** situations, you **continually** waver back and forth and **cannot come** to any '**clear**' decisions. Inside you are irritable, **chaotic**, and try to create an outcome forcibly. You do not **consider** that it is you who has **created** the inner barriers that you **continuously come** up against and that hold you back. You **cry** about lost **chances**. You tend to **care** for others, forgetting the **commitment** to yourself and **cling** to old beliefs such as 'I have to' or 'I should'. When you **cure** yourself of the past, doors to new experiences will not be **closed** anymore but open wide for exciting **challenges**. Now it's time for a **change**. Free yourself from debilitating **chains**! Become **conscious** and **courageous**!

In the positive **C** and **2** phases, you recognize that you are the **center** of your reality, the main **character** in your 'personal' **cabaret**. You are also a **catalyst** that inspires your '**co-players**' to find their **capacity** for joy. You **check** what does not suit you anymore and **consider** the **changes** needed in your life. You are **certain** that you are **capable** of **creating** a wholesome reality from one day to the next. Like an uninhibited **child**, you **concentrate** on the positive. You **choose challenging** experiences and **caring** friends with whom you share inspiring **conversations**. Your vision is **clear**, and you see the happy aspects of life. You are **charismatic** and **charming**. You **celebrate** yourself and life's marvelous moments with a glass of **champagne**.

D / 3

DANIELA, DARREN, DAVE, DENIS, DIANA, DONALD, DOROTHY, DYLAN…
DENMARK, DUBAI, DAMASCUS, DELAWARE, DALLAS, DUBLIN…
DISC, DIARRHEA, DEMENTIA, DIABETES, DEPRESSION…

D and 3 stand for you daring to step out of the dark into light.

The **3**-year-old child begins to **distance** himself from his center, which brings about the first **debates** with others – siblings, parents, etc. The child now learns to **defend** himself as well as to stand up for his **desires defiantly**. He is **discovering** the world. A new day is **dawning**.

Negative **D**'s and **3** phases shake you awake. Very often, you are faced with thoughts or stories of **death, danger,** and **disaster**. You tend to be **de-pressive** rather than pro-gressive. You feel **dull** and engulfed in **darkness**. You don't realize that everything that is happening comes out of your thinking. It is the mirror of your inner world. You rather try to **duck** away and **denigrate** yourself instead of **declaring** your own needs. **Despondent** and **dejected** you live a **disciplined** life. A sense of **defeat** always is accompanying you because you give your power away and are **dependent** on what others tell you. You are **divided** in yourself as you do not uncover your **dark** and unconscious sides. Now is the time to see the **delusion** in your thinking, to make **decisions** for yourself, and to **dare** to **declare** what is right for YOU! Be faithful to yourself and believe that your **dreams** become a reality!

In positive **D** and **3** situations you have gone through the **dark**, through a '**death**' so to speak and now feeling reborn, you see the light everywhere. Spirit, soul, and body are in harmony. You are **discerning** and perceive life from a positive, elevated point of view. You **devote** yourself to the search for inner **depths**. You are not **dependent** anymore on the opinions of others but **decide** for yourself. You also **dare** to speak up for what you want. **Dauntlessly**, you step through open **doors** into new experiences as you know that they will bring up **dazzling** aspects of yourself. You no longer approach people distantly, but openly because you know that they illuminate the **dark** sides of your 'I'. Now you **dedicate** yourself more and more to **deserving** friends with whom you communicate **directly** and share **deep** moments. You break through **dams** to let your inner being flow and are looking forward to a **delectable** life – a life that is a journey full of **discoveries** – it becomes a **delicious dance**!

E / 4

EDDIE, EILEEN, ELIOTT, ELISABETH, EMILY, EMERIC, ERROL...
EUROPE, ENGLAND EGYPT, EQUADOR, EL SALVADOR, EDINBURGH...
EYES, EARS, ELBOW, ESOPHAGUS, ECZEMAS, EPILEPSY...

E and 4 stand for using your energy to end that which no longer serves you and encourage the new.

In general, it is a phase of an **exit** out of **emptiness**, and thus of **expanding** and **emancipation**. The 4-year-old child **emerges** into the garden to play on his own. For you, it means to step into the '**external**' world. Now you need to **expel** and **efface** old thinking and behavior patterns and let your **energy** run free to **explore** the new.

The negative **E**'s and **4**'s symbolize that you do not use your **energy** for a change. Your life seems **empty**, and you feel tired. Afraid of making **errors**, you would rather **escape** than **energetically** move forward. As you see the **evil** side in everything and everyone, you **encounter enemies** as well as **egotistical** people. You are **entangled** in a net of fear and narrowmindedness, which can only be **effaced** when you choose to step out of it. By wanting to **extort** your goals with your head, you **expend** your inner **energy** wrongly and get **exhausted**. **Enough is enough**! You finally need to be honest with yourself to live a truthful **existence**. Claim your space and live up to your authentic 'I', the positive quality of the '**EGO**' that says: I am important, I matter! **Energize** yourself – **embark** on a new journey!

The positive **E**'s and **4**'s phases bring you the long-awaited success, **excellent** results, and the harvest of your **efforts**! You have learned to be the center, are independent, and you use your **energy** now for yourself and your **evolving**. You **express** yourself clearly. You **experience** situations with full **enthusiasm**, and seeing that which is **essential**, you **endorse** a new **exciting existence**. **Enlightened**, you now give your inner baby **extraordinary** opportunities to **enjoy**. Your **self-esteem** is strong, and this **enables** you to **embrace** the positive **echoed** back to you. You are **empowered** and have become an **elegant entrepreneur** in your life. Whatever you materialize **emblazes** you because you **embrace** the **elixir** of life. Your **energy** is **endless** and brings you astonishing and **enormous** great opportunities to further **expanding**.

F / 5

FAYE, FELIX, FLORENCE, FLOYD, FRANK, FRED...
FRANCE, FINLAND, FLORIDA, FLORENCE, FRANKFURT...
FEET, FINGER, FACE, FOREHEAD, FLU...

> To feel fresh, free, and full of energy. Having fun is the highest goal. **F** and **5** connect you to it. To experience freedom and joy while being flexible.

In negative **F** and **5** phases, you are caught in the **frustration** of the daily routine, of **financial** worries and **fixed** beliefs. You **feel frozen** and no longer **free** to move forward into a fulfilled **future**. You only see the **faults** in others without looking at your **false** illusions. Keeping company with old-**fashioned fellows**, you **forget** your desires and **flee** your responsibilities instead of **following** opportunities to move **forward**. It's time to remove the **frustrating fetters** that you have placed on yourself – those that inhibit your freedom to live **fully**. You must learn to trust and have **faith** that you are **fit, flexible**, and **fearless** enough to build a **fertile foundation** now and break through the **fences** that stop you from **fulfilling** your original goal in life, which is to **feel freedom** and have **fun**!

In the positive phases of **F** and **5**, you have **found freedom** and the inner **fellowship** with yourself and others. You have learned to have **faith** in yourself and stay **faithful** to yourself all the time. Since you are happy, you know that you will bring **forth** an exciting **future** as you know that you create it off your inner Self yourself right now. You have **freed** yourself from pressure and **flow** in a **fresh, free**, and happy way of living. Your knowing that your new thinking: 'me **first**' not only brings **fortune** to yourself but also to your **fellow friends** is **flabbergasting** and **fascinates** you. You are **full** of energy, and your will to go **forward** is set **free**. You **focus** on the **fruitfulness** in all there is and **feel** your inner **fullness** expressed everywhere. Your life is **fulfilled, fantastic**, and has become a non-ending **fizzed feast**!

G / 6

GABRIELLE, GARRET, GAVIN, GEORGE, GERALD, GIL, GRACE…
GREENLAND, GREECE, GEORGIA, GENEVA, GENOVA…
GALLBLADDER, GASTRO, GENITALS…

G and 6 stand for seeing the good in everything there is and thus generate glorious moments!

In negative **G** and **6** phases, you walk on a **grungy ground** and carry old **garbage** with you what makes your life dull and **grey**. You **grant** yourself neither **grandness** nor fun but tend to **grieve** over lost chances. Not seeing the **good** aspects of your life, you rather concentrate on the bad memories. Spiritually and physically, you repeatedly reach your limits, and often, instead of **going** forward, you are forced to **go** back or even **give** up. You create yourselves **gods** who are '**greater**' than you, and since you do not believe in yourself, you let them **guide** you. As you feel small and **guilty**, you do not see the many open **gates** that lead you out into real life. It's time to find back to your original **grandeur** by cutting away the **grids** you are caught in. Dare now to move and **go** – **go** and make a step forward!

When you have reached the positive **G** and **6** phases, you know that you are **good** and **generate great** opportunities that **generally** bring you and your **growth** forward. Your **genial** sides are revealed, and your earlier self-**generated gates** lifted. You can **get** enthusiastic about a thing or a person now again without **giving** up yourself. You can, therefore, **generously give** as you are also **gracious** and **generous** to yourself.
    You are very **glad** to live, know that you are **glamorous**, and **gather** friends around you who love your company. Knowing that you have **got** the **gear** in your hands, you lead yourself into situations where you can **grab** chances for your **glorious goals**. **Golden** and **gorgeous** times are ahead!

6 – six is close to sex through which something new, a new life is created. When you are aware that you yourself are the creator of your reality, you can realize something that has never existed before. You can be sure that your **genuine** abilities and **grandiosity** will work deep within you and will always bring you happiness and a **good** future.

H / 7

HAILEY, HARRIET, HAARY, HELEN, HENRY, HUGH, HUMPHREY...
HOLLAND, HELGOLAND, HAWAII, HELSINKI, HAMBURG...
HEART, HAIR, HERNIA, HAND, HIP, HEEL, HEPATITIS, HERPES...

Stop hoping but heartfully heading into happiness – this is the theme of H and 7.

Hops and malt are lost. This is the attitude in negative **H** and **7** phases. Out of this desperation, **hatred** arises out of love, both on the outside and, even worse, on yourself. You feel incapable of action and **hang** around in your old **habits**. Because you are spiritually **hardened**, you are confronted with **hard**-minded and **heartless** persons who **harm** and **humiliate** you and don't **help** you when you need them. You **hold** on to old believes and structures which do not give you any real **hold** but prevent you from shaping **heaven** on earth. It is you who is not **honest** with yourself, **hide** your true Self, and **hesitate** to speak out. Do not wait for a **hurricane** to shake you up as it's time now to get rid of your inhibitions and jump over obstacles and **hurdles**. Think of your **heart**!

When you **have** reached the positive **H** and **7** phases, you are **harmonious** and have found 'home', your safe **harbor**. You **have healed** old wounds in your **heart** and feel **healthy** and **handsome**. You always see the **half**-full glass! **Hearing** your inner voice, you find **hidden hints** in yourself that **help** you solve problems or climb **hills**. You are living in the **here** and now. And you control every situation even if you **handle** many activities in parallel. You **honor** and **hug** yourself after having done your **homework** by the change of your attitude. Since you are **happy** now, your life is full of **highlights** which makes you celebrate each day like a **holiday**. Feeling young, you dare to unrestrainedly aim **highest** goals – to create your **heaven** on earth.

Therefore you are **hot** on **hot** life experiences!

I / 8

IAN, IKE, IRENE, IRIS, IRVIN, IVOR...
ITALY, INDIA, INDONESIA, IDAHO, ILLINOIS, IOWA...
IMMUNE SYSTEM, INTESTINE, INFECTION...

I and 8 stand for your listening to your inner voice and for your irrevocably standing up to your I, the 'I am important'!

The **8 indicates** that you must learn to combine above and below, **inside** and outside. You all have an **inner** Self with **ideals**, **impulses**, and **ideas** which you should not atrophy but allow.

In negative **I**- and **8**-phases, you feel empty **inside** because you are **imbalanced** and doubt your **integrity**. As you believe in your **imperfectness** and **impotence** to alter yourself, you are **introverted** and **inhibited**. **In** vain you try to give your best when you let **impose** tasks from people who you think are **impressive**. You often even get **insulted**, which can make you **inevitably injured** or **ill**. You tend to be **impatient** but do not reach your goals as your beliefs in 'old' **institutions** and **idols** throw you back. It is time to **interrupt**! Do not ignore your very **important** 'I' anymore! You are, as everybody else, an **individual** with unique qualities! Stop now being **immobile** and **ignoring** your **inner** Self but start to believe in your **inner** baby, which will bring you new **insight** and **improvement** in your reality. Stand up to your 'I' – the **immortal** center around which all circles.

In the positive **I**- and **8** times, you have learned to know how **important** your 'I' is as you are the center and the creator of your reality. Having opened your **inner** 'world' new **impulses** from within and from without are coming towards you. You can realize the connections **intellectually** and to act **intelligently** according to these realizations. Now you stand by to your **intuitions** and **ideas**, pass them on and thus awaken **interest** in others and **inspire** them. Because your **initial** fire has **ignited** again, you take the **initiative** and no longer live isolated from the lifestream. You believe in your '**I** can' by which your self-confidence and self-esteem have grown, and you say '**I** am and **I** stand fully and completely by myself'! This attitude opens the way for an **interesting**, **intense**, and **impressive** life.

Y / 9

JACK(IE), JAMES, JAY, JENIFER, JESSICA, JIM, JOHN...
JAPAN, JEMEN, JORDAN, JERUSALEM...
JOINTS, JAUNDICE, JAW...

J and 9 stand for your finding back to juvenility and having joy.

The planet **Jupiter** symbolizes expansion and happiness, **joy**, and **jubilation**.
The **9** is the last number before the **jump** into a new dimension.

In negative **J** and **9** phases, you feel **juiceless** and live your life **joylessly** as you believe that you are too old and thus resist to make any change. You rather **join** the same friends at usual places and **jabber** along instead of daring to go on a **journey** into new territory and experiences. You are against everything that is because you are basically against yourself and repeatedly act against yourself since old negative memories **jam** you. In your thoughts, you are in **jeopardy** and **jitter** to be **jobless** or alone, but on the other side, you tend to **judge** people and to be **jealous**. The **jar** of negativity is full now! You need to give yourself a **jolt** and **jump** out of your self built up **jail** to find back to your **jauntiness** and **juvenility**. Start to move forward now and become open for the **joys** life will offer to you when you say Yes to yourself!

In the positive **J** and **9** times, you have rediscovered your **juvenility** and **jollity** again! Since you concentrate on the happy aspects of every day, you take your mental **journal** full of positivity into sleep. Therefore you find **joyful** reasons every moment to **jump** up like a vigorous **Jaguar** and cheer. Feeling like a **junior** you **jauntily** be open for new **journeys** since you know that whatever comes will bring you more knowledge and wisdom. Each new experience promotes your consciousness and exposes your great multidimensional Self. Now you say '**JA**', YES to yourself and to what you have created inwardly and **jubilate** at the beautiful **jewels** that echo back to you!

K / 10

KAYLEE, KATE, KEATON, KEITH, KEN, KEVIN, KIMBERLY...
KENYA, KUWAIT, KANSAS, KYOTO...
KNEE, KIDNEYS, KNUCKLE...

K and 10 stands for grabbing the keys to open doors for more knowledge

In negative **K-** and **10**-phases, you feel mentally and physically '**knackered**'. You lack concentration and clear thoughts because you are hanging in the **knots** tied by yourself. Nothing wants to succeed, no person loves you, and life appears to you as struggle and cramp. You **keep** on believing and behaving in old structures and implicate yourself more and more in a downward spiral. As a result, you often are **kidded**. You have to **kneel** like a **knave** instead of courageously dare to step over the curb into uncharted territory.

Now, however, a new circle begins, symbolized by the number **10**. You must realize that you have already **known** and experienced many things in the past. So you can't be catapulting yourself into a catastrophic life with miserable 'I can't'. Be **kind** to yourself! **Kick** yourself and say 'I can', and I want to! Take the **key** and discover your fantastic core.

In positive **K** and **10** phases, you have dissolved the **knags** and **knots** of the past and are **keen** on making new experiences. You have gathered a great deal of **knowledge** and **keep** on searching for more.

You have learned to be **kind**, cordial, and respectful towards yourself and others. Like a child, you say 'I can'! With the awareness of this inner power, you become a true life artist and can master all situations with little effort. Always using your **key** to get in contact with your unconscious side, you are **keen-witted** and conscious of your **knacks** and skills – you proudly walk through life like a **king**. Fascinating moments and interesting people **kindle** you up; you often feel yourself like a dancing **kite** flying in the sky. By looking at things from above, you can recognize the connections and **knit** a holistic picture. You have built up self-confidence, have found your marvelous inner **kernel**, and let yourself glide safely on the waves of life with your sturdy **keel**. You love and **kiss** yourself for being alive!

L / 11

LARRY, LAURA, LEILA, LENNY, LESLIE, LEWIS, LIONEL…
Portugal, LOUISIANA, LONDON, LUCERNE, LIVERPOOL…
LEGS, LIVER, LUNGS…

L and 11 stands for love and the lust to live.

Life is in contrast to the death movement. That is why people are so attached to life. But many **lack** what makes life worth **living**! Recognize what **love** and **life** mean – and joyfully accept the tidbits that you realize yourselves!

The negative **L** and **11** state is the result of **learned** faith patterns and old **laws** that negate and deny your true 'I'. This makes you **long** for affection or people and forget that first of all, you have to **learn** to **love** yourself now and become happy and alive. You are trapped by **lassos** and thereby **limit** the **living** within you, which is why you cannot freely **let** yourself go. You **live** mentally and physically on a **low level** and at the **limit** as you **load** unnecessary burdens upon you. Although you are surrounded by so-called friends, you feel **lonely**. You are **locking** yourself out from joy and fun. As you **listen** to others, you overhear your inner voice, which admonishes you to finally **learn** the **lesson**, to change something, and to recognize your needs first and foremost. Become open for your **long lost** inner Self!

In positive **L** and **11** situations, the school of **life** has brought you so many positive experiences that you feel **landed** on safe ground. You now trust yourself and know that you can **let** 'it' happen. You are alive and **look lightheartedly** forward to what you will create yourself next! Since you have reached **liberty** in your thoughts and your **life**, you always are **loyal** towards yourself and to others. You have **learned** that it is only possible to truly **love** when you have first built the **love** for yourself. For this reason, **love** radiates to you from everywhere, and **loving** and **largehearted** friends share your life. With your inner **light**, you bring **luminosity** and a happy **laugh** into all situations that **logically lead** to a **lot** of even more **lustful** moments. Your life is full of **love, luck, and luxury**!

M / 12

MADISON, MARC, MARIA, MARINA, MARVIN, MATHEW, MIKE, MORRIS…
MALAYSIA, MOROCCO MAINE, MARYLAND, MICHIGAN, MIAME, MUNICH…
MIGRAINE, MUSCLE, MOUTH…

M and 12 stands for the realization that each person is mentally the maker of matter.

In **M-** and **12**-phases, it is **mainly** about the topic of **making** and thus about the **male** principle, which every human being has half in himself. There are two planets whose names begin with **M**: **Mars** symbolizing this male forward thrust and the will to change and **Mercury** that not only is seeing what we **mentally** have to alter but also stands for the skillfullness of sharing and communicating. And then there is the **Moon**, the light of the night, wanting to encourage you to illuminate the other side of the **matter** and **makes** you aware of your womanly inner Self and **motherly** instincts.

In the negative **M-** and **12**-state, you surrender your power submissively. Since you want to keep up your 'good' **manners**, you confront yourself with the 'I **must**…' all the time, what makes your life **modest** and **miserable** and yourself **moody**. You cannot excuse the **mistakes** of others nor yourself. Concentrating on the **material** side and old **memories**, you **miss** the contact to your inner baby that begs for finally being heard. Not knowing what you want and what is essential for yourself, you are content with a **minimum** and say **maybe** or I **might** instead of **making** up your **mind**. The **moment** has come to let old **moral** commitments behind you and put your '**me** first' in the center of your thinking. You have to understand that the outside **mirrors** your inside. Thus it **matters** a lot that you **make** something – no **matter** what, but something that catapults you out of your **misery** and **makes** you happy again! You are the **maker**, and you have the power to change!

In positive **M-** and **12**-phases, you **manage** your life and are **mobile** to **move** forward. You have found back to your **middle** and put yourself into the **middle** of your subjectively considered reality. Nothing is more a '**must**' anymore because you have noticed how you can **make** the best of everything with your changed attitude. Spiritually and **materially,** your being becomes richer. **Many meaningful** possibilities open up, and you now dare to communicate your **main** wishes and needs openly and honestly. The **momentary** is vital to you because you know that you are **materializing** the future from it. You are the **maker**! You **magnetically** attract **mutually motivated** people with whom you **march** forward on your **motional** path in life. You are open to the **maximum**. And you are **mesmerized** by the **many magnificent miracles** that are **mirroring** your **magical** inside!

N / 13

NANCY, NATALY, NICHOLAS, NOAH, NORMAN, NORA…
NEW ZEALAND, NEW FUNDLAND, NAIROBI, NEW YORK…
NAILS, NAVEL, NECK, NERVES, NIPPLES, NOSE…

N and O stand for noticing that each point of nowhere or nothing asks for the opening to something new. Nothing is what does not make sense – double negation makes everything positive.

In the **negative N** and **13** times, it is above all important to **notice** the general **negativity** towards oneself and everything that is. It ultimately leads to **nothingness**, misery, and the belief that everything is useless. Become aware of how often you say **NO** without thinking, and thereby exclude yourself from the beautiful sides of life. For far too long, you have been thinking and acting **negligently** towards yourself, have told you '**never** again' so often but still have fallen back in your old structures. **Now** learn to put a yes into words – YES for yourself. Also use your will to separate yourself from **negative** thoughts, people, and situations. **Neptune**, the God of water, begins with **N**. On the one side, he stands for the veiled, **nebulous** ignorance, but also the primordial instinct, the creative and the infinite. **Neptune** calls you to turn the grey mist into the opposite, **namely**, sunny life! Be alert and **note** the **necessity** to stand to your **needs** in the **numerous** situations your inner Self is creating for you and make a change!

In positive **N** and **13** phases, you have changed your thinking and your beliefs. You **now** experience **new** situations and ascend into **notable** higher (or deeper) dimensions, from where you can grasp contexts better and will expose the unconscious more and more. You are **newborn**! You dare to open yourselves to other people '**naked**' and **naturally**. You are curious and '**naive**' in the positive sense; that is, you trust uncritically and unconditionally like a child, and on the other side, **nobly navigate** your life always being concentrated on the here and **now**. You **nourish** your inside. Thus you also integrate the positive side of **negativity** – the feminine, the receptive, and the receiving. You **nimbly notice** the **numerous nooks** that you **need** to lighten up to combine the **negative** with the positive. Then in everything, **nothingness** becomes essential since it is everything – like the darkness of the **night** that lightens your day! You have found back to your **native** I and your **nirvana** – how great!

O / 14

OLIVIA, OLIVER, ORIANA, OSCAR, OSWALD...
OMAN, ORLANDO, OHIO, OKLAHOMA, OREGON...
OVARIES, OVERWEIGHT...

The theme of O and 14 is to go out, jump over obstacles, and to be open and optimistic.

With **O** begins '**Oh**' – the exclamation of wonder and amazement, as well as '**OM**' – the **original** supernatural sound according to Hindu faith. Therefore **O**- and **14**-situations have to do with **openness**.

In negative **O-** and **14**-phases, you concentrate **on** the **outside** and are **obedient** to **others** because you have forgotten your real **obligations** to **obey** your inner Self. You sacrifice yourself, are **overactive, overworked**, and thus feel '**old**' and unable to break **out of** the **often** repetitive situations. You lock yourself up – are not ready to take a step **out of** routine and thus don't **open** yourself to a new circle. Your inner baby is now asking you to take a position determination and to **order** your thinking and re-**organize** your life. Instead of continuing to let your heart suffer and reacting **offensively**, you should now keep your eyes and ears **open** to tackle the **occasions** to jump **over obstacles** and to grasp the **opportunities** for a change of your **oppressing** thinking and behaving structures revealed.

In the positive **O** and **14** times, you have found an **oasis**, a fertile area, where you can move forward **openly** and **optimistically** and have your **own opinion**. You have learned that you are 'very important' and that you have **obliged** to be faithful and respectful to yourself. Your thinking is **objective** and **original**. Knowing that you are the author of your theater, you always spontaneously say **okay** instead of a 'no'. You **organize** your life **optimally**. Since you have integrated your '**obscure**' inner world, you have reached an **overview** to **observe** the many **open** doors leading to the **ocean**, which is filled with **opportunities** to bring out the **optimum** for a happy **opulent** life. You are **omnipresent** in each situation, and you see the **obvious.** Now you feel **one** with all there is! – What an **orgasmic** state of being when you have found back to your **origin** again!

P / 15

PATRICIA, PATRICK, PAUL, PENNY, PERCY, PETER, PHILIP...
Portugal, PARAGUAY, POLAND, PERU, PARIS, PENNSYLVANIA...
PENIS, PROSTATE, PANCREAS, PAIN, PNEUMANIA...

P and 15 stand for the affirming of your potential, your power, and thus for you to be positive.

In the Tarot **15** (XV) is the card of the devil, the adversary of the good, the antithesis of God.
A **person** or thing can only 'bedevil' you as long as you are unaware of your **potency** and **potential** – your creative **power** that creates your reality with all the **possibilities**.

In the negative **P**- and **15**-state, you **parry people**, your **parents**, **partner** or the **priests**, and much more. In your daily **play**, you **passively** let yourself be forced into a **part**, a role that you accept only for lack of your independence. This always leads to **problems**, **pain**, and often to **panic**. You stick to **principles** and **paragraphs** and thus **paralyze** your movement. You **plea** and **pray** for better times in vain, but **punish** yourself by being more **polite** to others than to yourself – you even **patiently** burden yourself with the **problems** of them. Now it's time to take a **pause** and make a **point** behind your 'old
poor' belief of yourself that you have built up in the **past** and liberate yourself of your self **produced prison**. A new **path** is opening with hundreds of **possibilities** to alter yourself **positively**!

In positive **P**- and **15**-times, you, like a **pioneer,** have opened up your inside **palace**, your other **pole** where you have found **peace**. And as the main **player** have built up your **positive place** where **prosperous** things happen. **Psychologically** and **physically,** you are doing well! You know of your **potential**, feel **pep** and **power**, and are **passionate** about everything. You see different **perspectives** and can bring everything **profitably** to a central **point**. This way, you are ready to make **plans** and **practically** realize them in reality – fantasies can suddenly become a reality! With the **partners** who 'fit' into your **puzzle** of life, you go and celebrate pulsating **parties**.

You know that **paradise** is nowhere else than here and now and that you can **program** it yourself.

Q / 16

QUEENIE, QUENTIN, QUINCY…
QUATAR, QUEBEC, QUEENSTOWN…

Q and 16 stands for quitting quarrels and for your opening up of your query of why it all happens.

The form of the **Q** shows that either something new is coming to you from outside or you are letting your inner being flow to create something new.

In negative **Q** and **16** phases, your innermost is hurt by 'attacks' from outside – just as **quicksilver**, a liquid metal, poisons your body. Since you let yourself be overpowered by the **quirks** of the others and try to stay **quiet**, you **quake** and **quiver** in your inside what sometimes leads to **quarrels**. You are surrounded by troublemakers, people who constantly complain and stubbornly insist on their rights. Now it's time to 'clean' and **question** yourself where you are unnecessarily torturing yourself. Do not stay in the **queue** and **quell** your exceptional Self anymore! Leave your **'qualms'** behind and **quest** yourself what you want and what you yourself have to change to make your reality better. So break out of the spiral of thoughts and situations dragging you down. **Q** and **16** are not about shallow problems, but about a deeper level of being. Something alive wants to break out.

In the positive **Q** and **16** times, you **queried** yourself of the why's and **quit** and **quenched** the negative thought programs. You have found your way back to the origin, the source, and the core of your being and are now ready for **quantum** leaps. Your new 'I' can now 'spring up' from the inner depths, step out and penetrate higher dimensions. You trust your inner baby and give life free rein because you know that in every moment, only the right thing happens for you. **'Quo Vadis'** (where are you going) is the **quiet question** you are asking your inner 'I'. This shows your new attitude towards life: I move forward dancing on waves and let 'it' flow. Spiritually you are lively and always realize the **quintessence**, the essential behind the appearance of reality. Your inner change makes your life a celebration of deep insights and joys filled with positive **quality** and **quantity** in everything.

R / 17

RALPH, RAVEN, REGINA, RIAN, RICHARD, ROBERT...
RUSSIA, ROMANIA, ROM, RHODE ISLAND, RENO, RICHMOND...
RECTUM, RIBS, RABIES...

R and 17 stands for: Realize and realize! Also, for responsibility and respect for yourselves and everything that is, and for recognizing and valuing your richness.

Red, the color of love and energy begins with **r**. If you love yourself and use your energy for yourself, you will be **rewarded** with **riches**.

In the negative **R** and 17 phases, your life is marked by **red** numbers, i.e., you are always in the 'minus'.
You give off your energy submissively and often have to **resign**. Like many others, you have been **raised** with **rigorous rules** through which you **restrict** your **real** life. Since you do not **recognize** your value, you do not **respect** yourself but throw away not only your spiritual but often also your material wealth to others. Caught in the daily **routine,** you **rarely remark** the positive mirrors in your **reality** but **rather** feel **rage** and want to **rant**. **Recognize** the burdens of the past that you have been carrying in your '**rucksack**' for so long! It's time now to become **responsible** for yourself, to **rearrange** your **rigid** thinking and behavior patterns, and **radically remind** yourself that you are the center and that the outside is the **reflection** of your inner Self. Dare to take a new **road** and to **revive** your life! Take the **right** look back, pick out the **raisins** from your memory, and make yourself aware of how **rich** you are in experiences and knowledge.

In positive **R**- and 17-times, you have learned what **respect** for yourself and everything else means. You value your **richness** and can share it with others without **regret**. You have gone through a long maturing process, and you can, as a **result, reap** the fruits of your efforts now. By being a **realist,** you very quickly **recognize** the **relativity** of situations and always take the **responsibility** yourself. You have **realized** that you are **realizing,** creating everything yourself and that you are the director of your life and can **reach** what you **request.** Since you are **rooted,** you are completely **relieved** and **receptive** to positive **results.** Your inner peace allows you to break through **rules** with a willingness to take **risks,** and you start something new with your energy. Your knowledge of your inner treasure, your **richness** will make you **raise** and become **richer** day by day – spiritually and real.

Now you can let yourself float on a **romantic river** while you are **rewarded** by the **reflection** of your inner **rising radiant rainbows.**

S / 18

SAM, SANDY, SCOTT, SIMON, SPENCER, STEVEN…
SWITZERLAND, SAMOA, SENEGAL, SAN FRANCISCO, SEATTLE…
SKIN, SCALP, STOMACH, SHOULDER, SPINAL COLUMN…

S and 18 are signs that you should build inner security and strength instead of continuing to cling to outer security.

When the **sun sets**, the light of day fades out, and you become responsible for the illumination of the night. Accordingly, in S- and 18-times, you are confronted with your **self-responsibility**, your inner **security**, and **strength**.

You see the **S** in all the drawings of the '8'. It **shows** the movement from inside to outside – the red color, which symbolizes the creating part of your **soul**. Your inner **Self** flows outward – makes reality.

In the negative S- and 18-state, the negative **side** of **Saturn** comes to bear: You are afraid and **secure** yourself – with insurances, with contracts, with keys and whatever. You are mostly under **stress**. By hanging in old **structures** and **sacrificing** yourself for others, you **stay** in the **shadow** and thus **stand** in the way of your inner **sun**, the center of your being. You **suffer** because you experience the **same sad situations** again and again. **Shake** yourself up now and **start** to **skip** the 'I **should**' and the 'I am **sorry**' – open your **shutters** and let the **stimulating signs** of the blinking **stars shine** onto you! **Sweep** away your old thinking and behaving patterns and **search** for the **sweet** things that **suit** you! Become **sure** that **Saturn**, who has the keys to open new doors, will be at your **side**. **Say** positive words and **see** all the positive aspects **surrounding** you now!

In the positive **S**- and **18**-phase, you have reached a **status** of inner **security** and **stability** that lets you **swing** – 'a **star** is born'! You have **searched** and found your **sunny source** of joy and luck. You **stand** on both feet in life, and by having built up your **self-esteem**, you feel **secure**, **strong** and **smart**. You know about your **skills**, have a **sharp sight** from a higher level, and thus **see** the **succession** of what **shows** itself in reality through your **saying** positive words. Your **smile stimulates** your **surroundings** and brings back many **surprises** to you. You **see** a more profound **sense** in everything, and even **strange** or **stunning situations** let you be one with your **soul** that constantly **spurs** you on. Your inner **Self** is in harmony with your 'I' what makes you **shine**, **sing**, and **swing** on wings up to the **sky**. What a **spirited**, **sparkling**, and **sexy** life that is!

T / 19

TAMARA, TED, TERENCE, THALIA, THERESA, TIM, TOM…
TUNISIA, TURKEY, TEXAS, TENNESSEE, TORONTO, TOKYO…
TEETH, THROAT, TONSILS, TONGUE, THIGH, TUMOR …

T and 19 stand for the trust in yourself and your temper to achieve triumphs.

The **tiger** starts with a **T** – the symbol of power and energy – use **them**!

Trapped and locked up animals, as well as humans, **tend** to languidly '**tiger**' around in their cages. **This** shows the negative aspect of **T** and **19**. You have **tamed** yourself because of the **thoughts** that **tell** you all the **time** that you have to be obedient and patient. Now you are **tangled** in your self built-up old nets and **torment** yourself because you do not **take** a **torch** and burn all the **trash** from the past. You **tolerate trespassing** of your inner **territory** by **troublemakers** what makes you often feel **terrible**. **Thereby** you live **thriftily**, are **torn** apart from your inner Self, and **throw** away your precious energy with which you could change yourself and your reality. Realize that you play the role of a marionette in your **theater** and use your **temper** to **try** something – whatever it is, but **try**! It's **time** for a **transformation** now **to torpedo** your **traditional thinking** structures and finally start giving yourself **tenderness** and a lot of **treats**!

In the positive **T** and **19** phases, you have learned to be **tender-hearted** and **true** to yourself. You have changed your **thinking** and dare to **toast** to yourself and your **talents**. You are **thankful** to yourself that you have passed many **tests** that brought you forward and **thus** do not mourn missed opportunities. You have **taken** over responsibility on yourself in all your **thoughts**, words, and actions and can **translate** anything to understand the real sense behind. An inner **transformation** has **taken** place that gives you not divided but concentrated energy to keep pushing yourself and others to put ideas into action. Doors are now opening to **transcendent** and **thrilling** new experiences. You live on your **terms**, **trust** yourself, and **tirelessly** search for more **treasures** in your inner Self since you know that you must meet your innermost in all its **totality to** reach your higher **targets**. This makes you **thriving** and lets you **triumph**!

U / 20

UNIQUE, UNITY, URBAN, URIEL, URSULA...
URUGAY, URAL, UKRAINE, UTAH, UPSALA...
ULCER, URTICARIA...

U and 20 stands for understanding and unfolding of your Self.

The planet **Uranus** begins with **U**. It symbolizes the sudden and the **unexpected**: strokes of fate in the negative and miracles in the positive.
In general, great **upheavals** and **unveils** take place in **U**- and **20**-times.

In negative **U**- and **20**-times, you lack the necessary overview – you continuously **undermine** your value and your energy, are **uncertain, uptight,** and **undecided.** You put yourself **under** pressure not to fail and let yourself get stressed by **ultimatums** from others. Don't wait **until** an **uproar** and **upheavals** force you to alter yourself. Now it is time to dive into the **underground** of your 'I' searching for the causes of everything **unsatisfactory**. Your hitherto **unused** Self is waiting to be finally discovered! Let go from the **usual** and the **unnecessary** and start to **unveil** and **understand** the **unknown**. It's only your **unawareness** that makes you **unfaithful** towards your true Self. You are important and the center of your life! **Unload** yourself from your old habits and **use** your inner fire, your will to **uplift** yourself! Dare from now on to **utter** what you want and look forward to the **unexpected** and **unusual**.

In positive **U**- and **20**-times, you have realized that if you want to reach an **upper** stage, you also have to explore the **underside**. Thus, you have **unafraid undertaken** the journey into your **unconscious** world to **unveil** the **unspoken** and the **unknown**. Through your **understanding** and bringing together of the two worlds, you have become a **unity** in yourself again. Having reached this stage, your original 'I' can **unfold** more and more. **Uncommitted** and **unerring**, you use your energy to **undertake** further steps into **unusual** territory, **uplifting** you to see the whole **universe** from an **upper** point of view. You know that you are **unique** on one side, but you are also aware of your multidimensional Self that mirrors in all there is. This **unlimited** wealth you carry inside makes you ready now for the echoes of opulence from reality, for **unusual** and **unbelievable** experiences. You are **utterly** happy and **unceasingly** open for **unexpected** moments of joy.

V / 21

VANESSA, VALENTINE, VICTOR(IA), VINCENT…
VENEZUELA, VIRGIN ISLANDS, VIRGINIA, VERMONT…
VAGINA, VEINES, VERTEX, VISION, VIRUS…

V and 21 stand for vitality and victory through recognizing your value.

The planet **Venus** begins with **V**. It symbolizes the female side – the receptivity and the constructive principle. In translation, **V**enus is the mother who assumes the responsibility to carry out the spiritual and to connect it with the matter.

In the negative **V**- and **21**-state, you are in a **vacuum**. Since you do not respect your **value**, you believe that you are the **victim** and therefore have to helplessly and **voiceless** accept your fate. Because you give power to the outside world, you let yourself be **vexed** by it and sometimes even have to endure **violation**. Realize that your **vision** is clouded what makes appear the **verity** in the wrong light for you. As long as you believe in your old **validities**, you will not reach harmony because you separate the outside world from your inside. Your inner fire, however, eventually erupts like a **volcano**! So now, take responsibility for yourself, **verify** your **viewpoint**, and recognize that you are enormously **valuable** because you are the maker of your fate yourself!

Change your **view** now, pay attention to the many positive things, and use your **voice** to **verbalize** only positive words in the future – your inner alternation will be **validated** in your reality with lots of **vivid** and **valuable** rewards.

In positive **V**- and **21**-times, you have a **vigilant view** and see **vantage** in every aspect of your reality. You have realized that everything on the polar reality has 2 sides and therefore, can be **visioned vice versa** as well. This makes you see **verity** from an elevated point of **view**. You also are **very** attentive to what you **verbalize** as you know how much power your **voice** has and what **vast** sequences can follow. Your life, in general, is **vibrating**. You are **vivid** and **vigorously** lead your **vehicle** 'with 1000 **volts**' into a **vastly visioned** future. Since you recognize your **value**, you **vanquish** any doubts and **vaunt** your **valor** to dare to jump over bridges into new and unknown **ventures**. You are full of strength, positive **visions**, and bubbling with **vitality**. Because you are sure of yourself, you can materialize your many **voluptuous** ideas and look forward to many **various visible victories**!

W / 22

WARREN, WENDY, WESLEY, WHITNEY, WILLIAM, WINNIE...
WHITE RUSSIA, WASHINGTON, WEST VIRGINIA, WISCONSIN...
WAIST, WRIST, WIMPERS...

W and 22 are about your recognizing your worth, your wealth, and to know what you want.

In negative **W**- and **22**-phases, you **wait** for a miracle that will change your life since you grieve about lost chances. Your thinking is over-**weighed with worries** and beliefs that the **worst** could happen. You feel **weak** and '**withered**' although you **work** so hard and yet do not see the **worthy** results. Thus, you **walk** on **wobbling** feet through life and see in everything the **wrongs**. **Wake** up from your **wooziness** now! Do not **worship** others anymore, but start to recognize your **wishes** and say **what** you **want** for yourself! Instead of constantly saying, 'I **would**' use the word 'I **will**' from now on! **Wash** away any **worries** and start to trust in your **worth** and **wealth within** yourself! Do not **waste** your time and energy anymore, but **watch** out for the **wonders** that happen every moment! Concentrate on a **world** view that does agree with your inner **warmhearted** and **wondrous world** that reflects in your reality all the time!

In positive **W** and **22** phases, you have learned to pay attention to the **words** you pronounce because you have realized that the **world** comes out of your **words** being the concentration of your thoughts. You have used **weapons** to break **walls** and opened your unconscious **world** that is filled with **wealth, wisdom,** and glory. When you are **wandering** around a deep **warmth** is **within** you **with which** you **wide** openly **welcome whatever** comes up. You see the **world with** different eyes since you use your **wings** for an overview and hear the **whispers** of your inner Self **wisely** telling you **what** is **worthy** in your life. Since you have recognized the logical connections in all there is, you are conscious of your **wholeness**. Thus the '**we**' as part of yourself becomes crucial. With your like-minded friends, you **wittily** and **wisely** exchange what each of you **wants** to make everybody's life **wonderful**, happy, and fulfilled. With your quality of a **wizard** and your **willingness** to **win**, you let you carry on **waves** of **well-being** to **wisdom** and **wealth** – **wow**!

X / 23

XANTHUS, XAVIER, XENIA, XIOMARA...
XALAPA, XIAMEN, XIANGYANG...

The theme of X and 23 is about your concentration – to bring everything to one point.

The **X** is like a 'crazy' + (plus). Together with the **23**, it stands for the ability to concentrate on the core of the matter.
X is the 22nd letter of the Greek alphabet and is pronounced as Chi. In Chinese philosophy, Chi is the circulating life energy that is thought to be inherent in all things. Thus, the more you concentrate, the more energy you can set free.

In negative **X**- and **23**-times, you disperse your energies and thoughts. This you best see when people forget themselves through alcohol and are no longer in control. Similarly, it can happen to you without alcohol. You lose the overview and the ground under your feet when too much is coming towards you. Then you thus become almost 'crazy'. Instead of concentrating on what is important now, you get bogged down in **x-fold** activities and lose your energy. In such times you will often meet egoists. You think that they are wrong acting like this. Realize now that they are mirroring you what you are supposed to learn now: to concentrate on yourself and on what is essential to you now. Therefore, start finding out what is central and of importance. There is no time – all happens at the moment. Out of this, your following reality is created by you. That is why it is so important to concentrate on the positive events and mainly the ones of the day in the '23rd' hour before going to sleep because you yourself create your next day and can thus change your reality to the positive.

In the positive **X**- and **23**-state, you seem to be 'crazy' for other people: You have changed inwardly, see the outside with different eyes, and act in new ways. You are wide awake and concentrate on the importance at the moment and see the meaningful core in every situation. You can have any number of friends or projects that you can easily reconcile because you have developed the ability to focus on one and then on the other temporarily. You know about your versatility and find it far too dull to move only on a single-track. You have learned to have a snap retreat when it becomes 'too much' for you, and then, after a short pause, filled with pulsating energy, retake action. Now you are so self-secure that you are '**xenophile**', which means that you are open-minded to all foreigners or all things foreign to you. This attitude helps you to dive deeper into yourself and enrich yourself and your reality with much that is new and simply incredible. You feel like an enchanted child at **Xmas**!

Y / 24

YASMIN, YOLANDA, YOSEF, YVES, YVONNE...
YEMEN, YORK, YUCATAN, YELLOWSTONE PARK, YUMA...
YELLOW FEVER...

Y and 24 stand for the YES! And for the opening to the 'top'. The recognition of the logical connections, and the bringing down these insights to the ground of reality.

As you can see in the design of the '8', **Y** and **24** are on a different level. Yet they are parallel with A and 0. During the phase of **Y** and **24**, the old cycle runs out while simultaneously a new one consciously or unconsciously begins. These phases always have to do with recognizing what you have to or want to finish. And for what you open up, that something new can materialize.

In the negative **Y**- and **24**-state, **you** are close to giving up. All your efforts seem to come to nothing, and the once set goal disappears into nothingness. **You** have ideas being destroyed by the outside with many ifs and buts. The 'I', the vertical line of the **Y**, lets itself be depressed by the V above it, i.e., you allow the '**YOU**' to overpower **you** because of **your** wrong faith patterns. **You yawn** and close your eyes like, translated, in the 24th hour when you fall asleep and thus are stuck in the **yesterday** and excluding yourself from life.

But your inner baby is **yearning** to be heard and **yells** at you now to wake up and give yourself a **yank**. It's time to recognize your discrepancies, to realize your **yearnings**, and to put into clear words what you want to change. This way, you are ready to say goodbye to your old 'I' and find back to **your young** radiating Self again. If you do not alter **yourself**, the necessary changes come to **you** from the outside, such as a dismissal or a separation. Open **yourself** now for **your** inner worlds – recognize, decide, and go changed into a new cycle of life.

Yin and **Yang**, the female and male principles in Chinese philosophy, start with **Y**. Only when you have united these two sides in **yourself**, represented by the upper V in the **Y**, can the 'I' (the line of the Y) move freely and openly and decide for something new. Outside and inside are in harmony – the bipolar reality, symbolized by the 2 circles of the '8', unites in the great unity, the 0. Then **you** realize that every moment is a zero point from which **you** creatively materialize the following.

In the positive **Y**- and **24**-state, **you** see the logical connections of what **you** are materializing into reality and where **you** are therefore ready to make changes. **You** decide with what or with whom you will want to start a new circle of life. **You** say **YES** to **yourself**!

You have realized that every '**YOU**' is an aspect of your multidimensional Self. **You** have united **your** in- and outside – **Yin** and **Yang** – and are in complete harmony. This makes you say **yes** to everything and happily embrace all there is. You feel **young** and awakened and full of inspiration. **You** notice how **your** head becomes a 'sieve' and allows **you** to bring **your** ideas and impulses to the ground of reality at any time. A single word or clear thought suddenly has the power to change **your** life immediately. So now true miracles are possible that surpass **your** previous ideas and ways of thinking – **yippee**!

Z / 25

ZACHARY, ZITA, ZOE, ZEUS...
ZAIRE, ZAGREB, ZURICH...
ZOSTER, ZYGOMA...

With Z and 25, you are ending a cycle, a zero, while you already have set the goals for the next circle.

In the night, between 24:00 (=0) and 1:00 a.m., the experiences and insights of the day are combined with your inner will to build the new day creatively.

In negative **Z** and **25** phases, you are 'closed', you lock the windows and doors and are trapped like in a cell. You spiritually go back by hanging on to the past. You are not living the here and now and receding from the new. You have become accustomed to stepping back and give priority to others. The reason for this attitude is your anxiety and your doubts. You wander without any **zest** nor goals in a **zigzag** through your life. In your thinking, the negative aspect is foremost in the foreground – also concerning yourself. Realize now that you will go on to be a **zombie** when you do not alter yourself. Remember that you are the author, the director of your self created theater. But you have to become the main character as well as the spectator! Only by putting yourself up to the **zenith** you have an overview and can change yourself and your reality. Close a 'zero' full of negativity now and dare to step into this new circle with self-security and love. You were born to experience joy and fun – live it!

In the positive **Z**- and **25**-state, you have put energy in the **zeal** for the truth in the past. And you are now full of **zest** for life, for a new circle. You know that you are the center of your world view and thus have reached a **zenith** on one of your circles. You are finishing the old while the new one is fulfilling you at the same time. With full concentration, you **zippily** can jump from one moment to the other and are confident and forward-looking and, therefore, ready to change any state you have at any time.

Knowing that with each new challenge, you become more conscious, you go forward back to your origin. The big goal you are approaching is to be the magician of life, to penetrate the reality, or better said, the illusionary world with your thoughts and to become the creator of something new. Be happy to have come so far!

Through these words, you have received many clues to recognize yourself and your magnificence. Acknowledge now your uniqueness, your multi-talented and versatile gifts – you are the creator of what expresses itself in your reality! You are everything!

You have found answers to your questions, and are ready to step into your inner worlds. Be happy about yourself that you have opened the gates with the key and changed your view. Not the matter has power – you are the maker!

Now it is up to you to take responsibility for your life and your reality. By asking 'why', you will find the answers to your personal questions – they are here and within yourselves. Play around with what you have read, and translate the mirrored outside into yourselves. With practice, you can do this more and more fluently, and you understand more and more from day to day – just like when you learn a foreign language.

The answers that you find are the wisdom that you must now consolidate through your experiences in the matter. The material world is the 'testing ground' where you bring your knowledge to the ground to store it inwardly. Only when you switch and rule with the new consciousness and new actions, do you free yourself from your old wrong thinking and belief structures and let your fantasies and desires become a reality.

Take care to grant yourself the necessary peace and to realize your present point of view so that you, strengthened and clear, can climb the stairs 'up' and 'down' into the depths of your Self.

Rejoice in your insights! Let your life become a thriller and go on searching for your true original 'I'! Explore the crime scenes, find the culprits, the outdated belief and behavior patterns, and pull them out of circulation through changed behavior. You will be able to move fresh, free, and happy and boundless!

Be new-greedy! And let your ego spirit you!

Your will for the forward, which each and everyone holds, is pure energy and origin of all being. Use it and create your paradise on earth! You will make it!

And now some remarks and encouragements on my part, what I changed through these texts in my reality. I still live in the same place, but today I move quite differently and see new things that I didn't notice before. Am I only materializing them now? Yes, I am convinced of that! My view has completely changed through the concentration on the positive and the exposure of my dark sides. So many positively minded people who smile and look forward to seeing each other again accompany me on my journey. They are all altering and ready to light up their lives from another side — it is fantastic to hear about their changes and their new life experiences — an echo of my own transformation!

It is also unbelievable how much has technically developed since 1991 that corresponds to the texts I had 'received' at the time. Especially the realization of realizing reflects in computer technology. Isn't it fascinating that today we have 3D printers that 'print out' matter based on data entered by the programmer? These are 3-dimensional objects such as joints, teeth, and much more. Translated: We want to realize our wishes and ideas, such as a cup. However, we notice that this materially printed cup has a hole on the bottom — it does not correspond to our requests. So, where do we start to look for the mistakes? In the printer? No! We ourselves have entered something wrong while programming and now have to reprogram our input. It is up to us — we have the responsibility for what materializes as an expression!

The moment we become aware through the expressed result of our 'wrong' programs, of the patterns of thinking, believing, and behavior stored for a long time, we can take an insight into our unconscious sides — change ourselves. We can learn to recognize our value and to become aware of our importance and responsibility being the center of our reality. We can also realize that positive words bring us joyful echoes, and therefore one or more wonderful colorful 'cups' are expressed.

I have also only now understood the symbolism of the 'language' of computers, which is based solely on 0 and 1. It led me back to the above texts of numbers, where 0 is the whole, and 1 is the 'I'. Is, therefore, each person, translated, an inconceivable computer, a 'mental' machine? A data and program processing system that has everything in it and which can materialize, solidify new ideas from outside or from within but, is also capable of erasing them again? Yes, this is how the movement in reality must work – enter and print, realize and realize.

The big difference, however, is that we have our own will – to do or not to do as we want. And then there is the example of electricity. In our homes, this energy can be called up via any power socket. It is solely up to our will and our taking action to activate the toggle switch to bring light into the dark – we are the makers, we decide for dark or light.

The English word 'compute' means to calculate, but also to make sense. And here, we are reminded again that everything that we ourselves materialize can be 'calculated' logically and makes sense.

In the computer, there is the 'Mother'- or 'Mainboard', which is the central, the circuit board, the carrier of building blocks. In this socket, further cards can be placed. This board must have been our original Self, pure and neutral. Our will to become aware of the all-embracing 'I' allowed us to put new cards, new programs, on this board from year to year – first those of our parents, then those of our fellow man, the animals, the environment. Through contact with our mirror images, we have internalized these and with the experiences, associated with them, they have become memories. This corresponds to the disc space integrated into the computer, where information, translated: our experiences, is stored. Did we once receive information from the parents, the 'conductors', like: Look, the table is hard, and you bump your head against it, so after 3 times of experience we have stored this as truth on our hard disk. Over time, the matter became 'firmer', and the belief in it became fixed programs. I suppose that teenagers, 13 years and older, often seem so complicated and rebellious to their parents because they are defending themselves inwardly to recognize reality as valid. At this age, they lose the childlike, the playful, and have to adapt to new external rules.

This data storage space unconsciously stores everything that we once learned and internalized. A good example is walking – in the beginning, we had to practice to move on 2 legs. Today we do this automatically and are not aware of how much our processor has to work to do for a single step. Actually, it's incredible what we do automatically. Even when we drive a car, our unconscious 'I' takes over the steering, braking, accelerating, and we can talk to our passengers at the same time, detached from this 'work'. Have we ever patted ourselves on the back for this?

Our thought-, belief- and behavior- patterns function just as automatically – they are stored unconsciously on our hard disk for a long time. The daily routine lets us fall into the same patterns, programs, again and again, if we are not attentive. We have to realize those restricting us and replace them with new positive programs. How in the computer the deleted, 'repressed' past can be made visible again by specialists. Thus, the famous: 'Positive Thinking' is not enough to change reality. The hidden 'poison dwarves' will catch up with us again and again, if we don't also act according to the new programs. Experience only brings us knowledge – by being stored in our inner computer as truth!

We have all experienced that dealing with a new program is a bit tedious in the beginning, but practice makes perfect! So how important it is to say goodbye to the old, the familiar and to break up into a new ground – to illuminate the dark in us, to accept it, and to realize how incredible we are.

I know today that all my 'WHY's' have spurred my will of finding answers to the question: what is the meaning of life. To illuminate my reality from another side has made my life so exciting and happy. I took responsibility for myself, built trust in myself, and transformed myself from a puppet to the maker – it's fantastic!

The author

Born in Samedan (close to St. Moritz) in 1947, Katia Ricklin spent her childhood and youth in Zurich, where she attended school, which she completed with the Matura. She completed her education with a Proficiency degree in Cambridge, and also trained as a secretary in Zurich. After her divorce in 1974, she worked as co-director of Otto Ernst AG until 1988. From 1989 to 1998, she acquired extensive knowledge of Bach Flowers, Tarot, Crystals, and Photography through self-study and offered consultations and courses on these subjects.
In 1991 Katia Ricklin received the present texts and pictures by media. In 2017 the impetus for a revision of the manuscript and the publication of the book followed.

novum 🔸 PUBLISHER FOR NEW AUTHORS

The publisher

> *He who stops getting better stops being good.*

This is the motto of novum publishing, and our focus is on finding new manuscripts, publishing them and offering long-term support to the authors.
Our publishing house was founded in 1997, and since then it has become THE expert for new authors and has won numerous awards.

Our editorial team will peruse each manuscript within a few weeks free of charge and without obligation.

You will find more information about
novum publishing and our books on the internet:

w w w . n o v u m p u b l i s h i n g . c o m

Rate this book on our website!

www.novumpublishing.com